ALREADY ON HOLY GROUND

ALREADY ON HOLY GROUND

*Experiencing the Presence
in Ordinary Life*

J. K. Bailey

Hazelden
Center City, Minnesota 55012-0176

Library of Congress Cataloging-in-Publication Data
Bailey, John
     Already on holy ground : experiencing the presence in
ordinary life / J.K. Bailey.
          p.   cm.
     Includes bibliographical references.
     ISBN 1-56838-107-7
     1. Bailey, John. 2. Spiritual biography. I. Title.
BL73.B35   1996
291.4'092—dc20   96-4893
                                                  CIP

Editor's note
     Hazelden offers a variety of information on chemical
dependency and related areas. Our publications do not neces-
sarily represent Hazelden's programs, nor do they officially
speak for any Twelve Step organization.
     The following authors and publishers have generously
given permission to use quotations from copyrighted works:
From *The Kabir Book*, copyright 1971, 1977 by Robert Bly.
Reprinted by permission of the author and Beacon Press. From
*The Child Within Us Lives! A Synthesis of Science, Religion and
Metaphysics*, copyright 1986 by William Samuel. Reprinted by
permission of the William Samuel Foundation.

CONTENTS

The truth is that
the place whereon you stand
is holy ground as long as
you are contemplating
the presence and the
power of God within you.

—*Joel S. Goldsmith*

Already on Holy Ground is a secret treasure that whispers, rather than shouts, its reminder that the Infinite is always with us, if we but notice. Like a seashell held up to the ear whose sound calls us to the ocean, J. K. Bailey's wisdom alerts us to our own capacity for enlightenment, transcendence, and love, for getting beyond egotism.

The delight is that he does so with such full-tilt honesty and compassion, gently debunking myths that attract—and waylay—spiritual seekers. Examining the myth of enlightenment itself, he writes, "In the depths of my being I'll know it has nothing to do with channelers of wisdom or genial guardian angels. I will grasp that awakening is really about what we ourselves experience—through grace." And addressing the myth that spectacular inner experiences are more spiritual than the glimpses afforded by ordinary moments, he notes, "But in waiting for the blinding light to find us, we ignored the tiny sparkle of a star in the night sky that could bring joy to the heart and help us remember the Divine." Bailey sees through the myths that say spiritual people never get angry, that they avoid intense feelings—that they must perpetually seek.

Drawing on his own long-term odyssey, Bailey brings the sacred out of the church and ashram and into Kmart, six-lane freeways, and the local service station. "The potential for light is as present with mechanics amid the grease and grime of the neighborhood Amoco station as it is with Zen monks at a monastery in Kyoto." We do not have to go elsewhere, he emphasizes. God is here: in the midst of our anger, in the thick of our need to control, in the marrow of our pain, in the hush of a perfect, uneventful moment.

Already on Holy Ground helps us discover magic in the present moment. It awakens us to the potential for transformation in our immediate experience, encouraging us to work *with* our human tendencies rather than against or despite them. And as we do, we have a chance to recognize that experiencing our humanness, flaws and all, is what allows the divine to peek through.

—*Naomi Rose*

First, I am grateful to William Samuel who taught me about glimpses, judgments, and spiritual wonder. He also taught me about the simple presence which changed my life.

Second, I am grateful to wise ones whose writings have guided me. Among them I owe special thanks to David Manners, Nisargadatta Maharaj, and Joel Goldsmith. Their words convey a truth that transcends the sentences on any printed page.

I'm also grateful to Charlotte Joko Beck, Eugene Gendlin, Fritz Kunkel, and Stephen Levine, whose books gave me new ways to explore the link between the psychology of everyday feelings and spiritual awakening. Thanks, too, to Stephen Wolinsky, whose recent work points so lucidly in the direction of "I am that."

In addition, I want to thank the following people who contributed to the book directly and indirectly in its various stages: Bruce Bayard, Zoe Becker, Laura Blake, Jim Curtis at the On the Wall gallery, Emily Kretschmer, Don Leeper, Alfred Lowman, Vince Oredson, Naomi Rose, and Rachel Samuel.

My thanks also go to the people at Hazelden Publishing—Dan Odegard, for his enthusiasm and creativity as trade publisher, Betty Christiansen, whose perceptions as editor were always valuable and on target, and manuscript editor Cathy Broberg, who contributed her expertise as wordsmith.

Finally, thanks especially to my best friend and partner on this tempestuous life journey. Kat Bourque wields her editor's pen with grace and skill. For her unfaltering support and love, I'm deeply grateful. Together we cry tears of sweet joy in the presence.

"I'm afraid we're going to have to let you go," he says, staring down at the cuff of his blue Brooks Brothers shirt. "I feel terrible about it. Let me know if there's anything I can do."

On this sweltering August morning at a weekly newsmagazine in Manhattan, my boss has just summoned me into his office. My world of *linguine al pesto* lunches at Barbetta's and a corner office on the seventh floor of a pale-green skyscraper in the west fifties is about to collapse. So is my career as a marketing manager.

But things aren't as gloomy as they seem. In a few days, the initial shock and worthless feelings wear off, giving way to a sense of unbounded joy.

For the first time in twelve years, I'm free of memos and meetings, free of corporate games and in-fighting. Soon I'll feel free to explore a spiritual world that from a distance I'd always viewed with suspicion.

My getting fired launches me on a journey of self-discovery that will last twenty years and transform how I think, act, and live. Before it's over, I'll practice yogic techniques of meditation. I'll discover the mysteries of Zen Buddhism and Sufi mysticism; I'll delve into Hindu and Vedanta texts. On a moment's notice, I'll drive thousands of miles to visit an enlightened recluse who, when he's not deciphering the mysteries of metaphysics, traipses the Internet. I'll trek to the Anza-Borrego desert near the Mexican border at midnight, where I'll watch in disbelief as a trickster of the occult disappears in the sand before my eyes.

Ultimately, I'll discover this quest—despite its visions, powers, and mystic phenomena—misses the mark. It's not what propels me on this spiritual journey. What I want is much simpler. The transformation I seek requires no effort, no pilgrimages, no vivid meditations, no gurus with charisma. Neither complicated nor flashy, it has little to do with New Age phenomena.

On the contrary. The answer will come from the tiniest part of my entire journey—simply *being* in the presence of the Infinite—the same gentle presence Brother Lawrence described in his spiritual classic *Practicing the Presence of God.*

I'll find out that not only is this presence real, but it's available to each of us in simple circumstances.

I'll learn about awakening to this presence. I'll find out that not only is this presence real, but it's available to each of us in simple circumstances. No longer will I view spiritual awakening as a remote event that occurs once in a hundred lifetimes. No longer will I reserve it for exotic Eastern sages or for wild-eyed mystic poets. In the depths of my being, I'll know it has nothing to do with channelers of wisdom or genial guardian angels. I will grasp that awakening is really about what we ourselves experience—through grace.

Still, all my spiritual activities aren't wasted. Amid the rituals and structured meditations something good is happening. I'll learn the futility of doing, questing, and searching. Eventually I'll realize that what I'm looking for isn't about *my* doing anything. I'll learn that I cannot find what I want in ceremonies or holy places. No black-suited minister or guru in a white tunic will give me the secret of experiencing the presence. For that I'll have to learn about effortlessness, about letting go.

I wrote *Already on Holy Ground* because I believe spiritual practice need not be complicated or exotic—that awakening to the experience of Eternity's presence can be surprisingly simple. There's no need for special training or rigid discipline. We don't have to live like do-gooders or saints. Ordinary people, unaware of theology or holy scriptures, without benefit of a single bead, cross, mantra, or yogic posture, can and do experience the presence all the time.

This book suggests that we can take our normal reactions to everyday life—our grief, joy, love, arguments, depression, disappointments, even our anger and heartaches—and use them all to experience the Eternal.

Already on Holy Ground offers a new way to look at spiritual practice, focusing on what *we experience* rather than on dynamic teachers, meditative techniques, or the benefits that come from living in what some call the New Age.

Bear in mind, I don't suggest there's anything inherently exciting about experiencing the presence. *Already on Holy Ground* offers no visualizations or techniques for recalling past lives, no *chakras* to balance. Readers accustomed to a spirituality full of magic and miracles may miss some of the spiritual fireworks. Except for a couple of paragraphs in the first chapter, there's little in this book about exotic gurus or occult tricksters who display shamanic powers.

That doesn't mean there's anything boring about coming into this presence. Far from it. As I've grown to love it more and more, a sense of wonder and tranquillity accompanies me. So, too, does a sense that life is unfolding perfectly. I'm not suggesting by this that I go around blissful most of the time. I don't. I'm as prone to grumpy moods as anyone. But as time goes by, I experience the presence more and more. And that has made my link with Eternity real.

At first you may find the idea of being in the presence too simple. For decades I didn't know it existed. Had I known, I also would have found it too simple. Convinced that cosmic lights and advanced meditative states were what spirituality was about, I ignored the presence, mistaking spiritual peripherals for the real thing. I was more interested in *doing* than in *being*.

Finally, I'd like you to know that I'm an eager, flawed experiencer of life—a shy, passionate, stubborn, sometimes angry twentieth-century writer who loves God. *Already on Holy Ground* is about my joy and suffering, my gaffes, my successes, my trials and adventures. It's about experiencing the presence in everything. Being in the presence has transformed my life. It can do the same for you.

PART ONE
AWAKENING TO THE PRESENCE

*At the core of spiritual life
lies a gentle presence.*

Chapter One
THE ENLIGHTENMENT MYTH

Late one Fourth of July evening in a Los Angeles auditorium, I watch a spiritual teacher perform a remarkable stunt. A striking figure in his mid-thirties, he is lean and long-limbed. He wears a tight-fitting jacket bedecked with turquoise sequins. His unlined face and the curls that cascade over his forehead set off round, luminous eyes, giving him an angelic look. But he is no innocent. A master of the occult, he displays the confidence of a rock star accustomed to crowds who hold him in awe.

As the lights dim, I look up toward the stage. My eyes squint. The occultist's clothes look transparent. I can see through them! Snippets of gold move in schools within the perimeter of his torso. Tiny sardines of light, they dart in elliptical circles, moving in staccato rhythms, like a constantly flashing Las Vegas sign. What I see astonishes me. I've never witnessed a human light show before!

———⟫·◦·⟪———

After lifetimes of strenuous seeking,
I believed I would awaken to that
timeless state where I'd experience
union with Eternity.

———⟫·◦·⟪———

My fascination with these supernatural powers reflects my spiritual journey then. In those days, I sought bliss amid white lights and spectacular mystical states. Always looking for the most intense spiritual experience, I would compare one teacher to the next. "He must be the right teacher for me," I'd think. "I looked around me and saw light permeating everything." Or I'd complain, "I didn't feel the *kundalini* move through me during that meditation. Maybe he's not *fully* enlightened."

Without realizing it, I had accepted the enlightenment myth, which suggests that *if* I meditate diligently enough, *if* I'm pure and unattached, *if* I'm sufficiently benevolent, *if* I find a fully enlightened teacher, *then* one day I myself will become enlightened. After lifetimes of strenuous seeking, I believed I would awaken to that timeless state where I'd experience union with Eternity.

As part of my quest, I visited ashrams and meditated at weekend retreats. I immersed myself in Vedanta and Zen Buddhist philosophy and investigated the Gurdjieff work. I exulted in the poetry of Rumi and Kabir and grappled with the logic of Krishnamurti. I studied the *Gita* and the *Tao Te Ching* and pored over the transcribed words of Nisargadatta Maharaj and Ramana Maharshi. I even plunged into the writings of Christian mystics, expecting to find them narrow-minded and dull. But the genius of Meister Eckhart and the pragmatism of John Chapman electrified me.

At the root of my search lay a selfish goal: enlight-enment. I wanted to awaken spiritually, to reach that magical union with Eternity. So the search was about *me*. The emphasis? Always on me, on changing, improving, empowering me. Although I told myself I was on a path to destroy the ego, this obsession with my own transformation expanded that very ego.

———⬥———

What was missing was spiritual juice. My spiritual practice was static, empty of aliveness.

———⬥———

What does "destroying the ego" mean? I believed it meant that one day I'd no longer think of myself as a separate individual. Egoless, all my worries would disappear. Lust, fear, greed, desire, and tem-per tantrums would no longer taunt me. I'd be unselfish and unattached. Self-perfection—that's what I was after!

With enlightenment, I'd become perfect. No longer would I feel shy around crowds. No more would I feel angry, afraid, hostile, controlling, or judgmental. My fears of cancer and its chemotherapy cures would disappear. So, too, would my needs. No more would I crave garlic and chili peppers on my pasta. No more would I yearn for fudge brownies or Pete's Wicked lager. Free of all attachments, I'd laugh off my desires like a holy Tibetan madman.

For twelve years I pursued the enlightenment myth with its promise of perfection. I did all the things I thought spiritual people did on their spiritual journeys. I chanted, prayed, meditated, and experienced flashy mystical phenomena. I put my faith in mantras and *yantras*, incense sticks, and Indian philosophers who claimed to have died to their egos. Yet despite all this, despite vivid meditations and visits to wise ones who offered answers to life's deepest mysteries, I felt uneasy. Something was missing.

What was missing was spiritual juice. My spiritual practice was static, empty of aliveness. Granted, I knew how to count my breaths, still my mind, and visualize serenity. I was also beginning to grasp the meaning of surrender and nonattachment. But none of this made me feel closer to the Infinite. None of it afforded me a taste of what I would eventually recognize as the presence. If I'm honest, I admit that when it came to God, I experienced nothing.

———⇒•⇐———

Yes, what really matters is experiencing the presence.

———⇒•⇐———

Looking back, the emptiness of my spiritual quest reminds me of an evening I spent in a hotel ballroom on Manhattan's West Side, listening to a dark-suited scholar with a sallow face and bulging briefcase define creativity. He methodically dissected every step in the act of creation. No sense of joy or spontaneity crept into his words. He allowed no room for mess or confusion.

"Creativity," he proclaimed, "is the quality of bringing into existence something new. It is characterized by originality and expressiveness. Would anybody like to give me their definition?" To each answer he alternately responded, "Excellent!" or "Very good." At one point my attention was pulled to the closest of four windows that faced the street. Five stories below, I heard the shriek of brakes and horns as cars and taxis wound their way uptown in the late evening. The screech of traffic refreshed me. Suddenly, I felt compelled to leave this orderly scene. Without thinking, I strode out of the ballroom and hopped into an elevator that took me down to the main floor. I made my way out through the lobby onto Broadway near 76th Street. Outside, candy wrappers and cigarette butts littered the sidewalk. I walked past a deli with a green-and-white Heineken sign, past a funky orange juice stand with browned hot dogs rotating in grease, down to the corner newsstand. I stopped and sucked in the night air, thankful that I was now experiencing life instead of trying to figure it out.

In the same way the hotel lecturer sapped the lifeblood of creativity by analyzing it, for years I had sapped the lifeblood of my spiritual journey by using my mind and its techniques to approach the Eternal. Every notion I had of the Infinite was logical rather than experiential. Others—saints and gurus, philosophers and metaphysicians—explained to me how my spiritual life should unfold. They interpreted holiness for me. Little wonder my spirituality was thirdhand! I read and heard *about* the Divine, but no book, teacher, or technique is a substitute for *experiencing* the Infinite.

Yes, what really matters is experiencing the presence. Otherwise, all the gurus and meditative techniques, all the rituals and pilgrimages are superfluous—hood ornaments for a well-designed car whose engine is missing.

When we discover the presence through our own experience, we don't have to prove God's existence to anyone. There's no need for special training or rigid discipline. No guru or rabbi, priest or minister gives us the secret of knowing God. When we recognize it within us, then we know that we know. We realize that what we're searching for has little to do with our efforts. We learn that what we want is to experience the presence. For that we only have to look within.

It's pitch dark out, a little after five o'clock one gusty October morning six miles southwest of Minneapolis. Into the trunk of my red Honda I load a faded green canvas bag stuffed with enough clothes for five days. On the right front seat I put a navy blue knapsack containing a packet of trail mix and two bags of peanut M & M's. In the zippered pocket of my knapsack, I place a copy of Lao-tzu's *Tao Te Ching* and an index card with some questions scribbled in a red felt-tip pen. The questions—about why people suffer and how to awaken spiritually—have obsessed me for years.

I'm about to set out on a 1,200-mile drive to the hills of central Alabama. I intend to visit William Samuel, a twentieth-century American wise one, a homespun philosopher who has spent decades deciphering the mysteries of metaphysics. I believe he may have answers to the questions on my index card. Though I don't realize it then, my questions will remain unanswered. Yet this journey will forever change how I view spiritual life.

After a stunning drive through four midwestern states whose leaves blaze with the fall colors of rust, scarlet, and burgundy, I arrive at the house of William and Rachel Samuel at around three the following afternoon. They live in a forties brick rambler east of Birmingham. Rachel Samuel greets me at the door with a smile and a southern "Hi!" In her early fifties, with blonde bangs that set off an observant, kind face, she resembles Jo Anne Woodward.

The door opens into their living room. Inside, nothing is as I have pictured it. Perhaps I envisioned a California-style spiritual retreat. But there are no candles, meditation cushions, or glossy photographs of Indian philosopher-saints—not even the scent of sandalwood. Nothing exotic in the slightest. On the right-hand wall, framed in gold, I see an oil painting depicting an Italian farm scene. It faces a white sofa and some easy chairs. On a low shelf, a twenty-four-inch Sony TV perches above a video recorder. A sturdy-looking exercise bicycle stands near the wall that adjoins the dining room.

Then I meet William Samuel. Bespectacled and gentle looking, he seems an unlikely candidate for my philosopher with all the answers. In his early sixties, wearing striped suspenders and a light blue denim shirt over a white T-shirt, he seems better suited to watching cardinals vie for sunflower seeds at a bird feeder. He doesn't look like the philosopher who has just finished a 400-page book synthesizing science, religion, and metaphysics. He shakes my hand and, after a minute or two of small talk, suggests we meet early the next morning in the cottage in back where I'll stay.

The cottage—the Samuels call it "Woodsong"—has a living room with cedar-paneled walls and smells like pine needles in a damp forest. There's a low bookshelf stained in walnut just to the right of the entrance as I walk in. I see four or five arrow-heads and some small pinecones scattered on top. Below, I catch a glimpse of a couple of titles: *The Zen of Seeing* and one of Stephen Hawking's books—I think it's *A Brief History of Time*. On the coffee table in front of the couch there are a couple of recent issues of *PC World* and a worn copy of *Calvin & Hobbes.* In the corner stands an antique rocker next to an old Franklin stove. The cottage feels cozy and lived-in, like a woodsy cabin in the Vermont mountains.

A little after eight the next morning, Samuel knocks on Woodsong's door and steps through the doorway, smiling shyly. After asking if I slept well, he sits across from me in an overstuffed chair on the left. I sit at one end of a long sofa across from a big picture window that looks out onto a grove of loblolly pines—pines whose loftiness gives them the quiet authority of redwoods.

We talk, at first about nothing in particular. I remember asking a question that troubles me: "Do you *have* to believe in God to be spiritual?" (By nature, I'm suspicious of religion, leery of those who talk readily of *God.*) His answer reassures me: "It's enough," he says, "to believe in the *possibility* of the Infinite." I feel relieved. Staunch belief isn't necessary!

———❖———

I'm aware of my mind getting quieter. My opinions and judgments begin to fade.

———❖———

As we talk, I look outside. Everything seems ordinary. Yellow leaves fall. Squirrels chase each other across the branches of tall oaks. Then I notice something unusual going on inside that rustic room. I'm aware of my mind getting quieter. My opinions and judgments begin to fade. I forget the outer world—my life with Kat back in Minnesota, the frustrations I've had editing a spiritual book. Forgotten, too, are the questions on the folded index card in my hip pocket, questions that only yesterday seemed urgent. I have no conception of time passing. I feel detached.

At this point, I sense that the couch I'm sitting on, the braided rug under my feet, Samuel, and even my own body seem less solid. It feels as if a pale gold haze descends over us, filling the room. Something seems to watch us while we talk; something witnesses what's happening. There's no need to think or do anything. Right now everything is unfolding perfectly. My eyes tear, perhaps because I've never experienced such a magic moment.

Just then, after this shift in perception, Samuel leans toward me and whispers aloud, "This is *it!* This is *it!* This is what people have quested for over the centuries!" His eyes are soft, wise from years of delving into the wonder of what he calls *it*.

What is this elusive *it* that Samuel speaks of? He simply means that Eternity's presence is there with us. His words reflect the transcendent hush that fills the room. Just then, I become conscious of the presence too. For the first time in twenty years of repeating mantras, counting breaths, praying to the cosmos, practicing yoga postures, and studying the great spiritual texts, I *consciously* experience being in the presence. And it happens without any effort—without doing anything at all!

———◆———

For the first time in twenty years of repeating mantras, counting breaths, praying to the cosmos, practicing yoga postures, and studying the great spiritual texts, I consciously experience being in the presence.

———◆———

In a letter months later Samuel would describe what we experienced: "*It* is a moment of relief from the world's heaviness. *It* is an instant of recognition, a weightless surveillance of the scene. *It* is a flawless moment that lets us say, 'Hey, this is a fine minute! I feel all right!' *That's it.* That goodness and light-ness is *it*. It's no big event to the intellect. Yet its recognition and acknowledgment is the most brimming inner understanding anyone will ever acquire—and the heart knows this is so. Suddenly everything is all right."

⎯⎯➤◦◄⎯⎯

Who would have thought the experience I'd sought for years was so ordinary, so much simpler than I'd imagined?

⎯⎯➤◦◄⎯⎯

On the surface nothing much is happening. Samuel doesn't mention "God," "truth," "Brahman," or "the Holy Spirit." He only says, "This is *it*." The only thing that happens on that October morning is that Samuel acknowledges the Divine. He acknowledges a transcendent moment—what he would later call a *glimpse*. Yet if Samuel hadn't pointed out the presence of *it*, I'd have ignored it. His acknowledgment was crucial.

Tears of gratitude fill my eyes. Who would have thought the experience I'd sought for years was so ordinary, so much simpler than I'd imagined? It had been with me, in me, all around me all along.

Chapter Three
THE MAGIC OF GLIMPSES

Something magical happens when we experience glimpses, those special moments when we're aware of Eternity's presence. We discover that spiritual truth already resides within us. What does "within us" mean? Simply that we don't need to look outside ourselves for this presence. Pursuit of books and teachers, techniques and philosophies in themselves don't bring us into the presence. Our own experience does.

Glimpses already exist in our lives. We've all experienced them. They're available in ordinary situations. Once we realize that the everyday stuff of life is what wakes us up, we don't have to do anything or go anywhere to find the presence. There's no need for repetition or elaborate rituals. We know Eternity based on what we experience ourselves. We can dispense with affirmations and visualizations. We can forget about reciting mantras and delving into our past lives. Why rely on holy scriptures or exotic teachers who live in Boulder and Bombay when the real teacher is within?

———————

Once we realize that the everyday stuff of life is what wakes us up, we don't have to do anything or go anywhere to find the presence.

———————

Because we don't know glimpses are special, we rarely pause long enough to notice and acknowledge them. "Moments like these," wrote mystic Paul Brunton in his *Notebooks*, "have come to many who have not recognized the preciousness, the special value, and uncommon nature of the experience."

Perhaps our twentieth-century Internet minds don't yet have a structure to grasp a notion that says we can access God *ourselves,* simply and gently, without intermediaries—without gurus and priests, without setting foot in a Baptist church, Zen temple, or New Age channeling center.

What follow are examples of glimpses. Notice that in each nothing important *seems* to be going on. There are no lights, no celestial voices, no visions or deep trances. Yet something *is* happening, something wondrous, something that gently shifts our perspective and transforms the soul.

As you read these experiences, keep in mind that what happens during a glimpse isn't as important as *our willingness to acknowledge it,* to affirm, "Yes, right now something special is happening."

RUNNING ON A SNOWY DAY

It's an early afternoon in late November. I'm running along Glenview, the forest road that winds along the mountain foothills high above Ashland, a village ten miles north of the California-Oregon border. As usual, during those first minutes, my mind also runs. "Did I start too quickly?" The tendon of my left heel begins to ache. I worry. "Maybe I ought to stop and stretch. Should I cut the run short?"

———⟫•◦•⟪———

It seems there's a watcher present.
It is an inner knowing.
Eternity is making its presence known.

———⟫•◦•⟪———

Soon snow starts to fall. The sky is placid and gray. A few snowflakes—the first I've seen this fall—melt on my eyelids and beard. I hear the hush that accompanies early snow in the forests of southern Oregon.

Farther along the road, I notice something subtle, something difficult to put into words. I sense a muffled stillness that seems to observe everything, that's quieter than even the snowfall's quiet. All around a detached silence descends. It seems there's a watcher present. It is an inner knowing. Eternity is making its presence known.

The infinite is here, present with me!

This Eternal perspective arrives gently. It is neither obvious nor dramatic. There is no hard evidence for it that I could offer a skeptic. I only know that I hear a soundless sound, like the sound of *om*, whose source is the source of stillness—the source of the universe itself. I acknowledge the shift in perspective. I'm grateful for experiencing the gentle presence.

For a moment I stop. I crouch along the edge of the road, my knees pushing into a dirt bank. From the zippered pocket of my windbreaker, I pull out a pen and try to scratch a few words on a scrap of paper. But the snowflakes smear my scribbles. When I struggle to record what I experience, the inner stillness leaves. But as soon as I give up writing, it returns.

The snow begins to fall harder. Now the sky is dense with white flecks. Irregular patches of white gilt the forest floor. From across the valley I hear the muted sound of a buzz saw coughing in bursts: *Eeeeeeeenh! Eeeeeeeenh! Eeeeeeeeeeeenh!*

But the quiet stillness continues its soundless presence. It offsets everything, even the din of the faraway saw.

———➤•◄———

My willingness to notice its divine
origin is what gave it its
special nature.

———➤•◄———

Below, a motorbike, its engine sputtering, zigzags up the hill. Still, the inner sound continues its hum. I look up and see a squat Chevy pickup from the Ashland Parks Department heading straight toward me from around a bend. Distracted for a moment by its closeness, I lose the inner calm. But it returns. A couple of snowflakes make a soft *fluhh* sound as they land on the wet brown leaves inches from my feet. I get up and start to run again, refreshed by a sense of exquisite calm, reminded of Eternity's presence everywhere.

When I look back on those moments during my run, I realize that I had no sensation of time passing. My personality—that usual sense of being me—receded. So did my perspective that "I am this body." I didn't notice my arms and legs or the ache in my left heel. I wasn't aware of my body at all. Instead my attention focused on a sense of a witness being there with me. Though nothing visibly happened, I was certain of the presence of Eternity.

Was the experience due to the spectacular forest setting, the quiet, the beauty, the feeling of timelessness? To be sure, those qualities were present. But that's not why I was conscious of the presence. The key was in how the experience was perceived. I could have viewed it as just a peak experience or memorable run in the woods during the late autumn. But by doing so, I would have missed its real significance. My willingness to notice its divine origin is what gave it its special nature. This acknowledgment took me beyond my John Bailey, me-oriented perspective and allowed the presence to come into my awareness.

In other words, it doesn't matter what happens— what the scene looks like or how we feel. What makes it special is how we hold it. What matters is whether we're willing to look at it from the view-point that something beyond exists.

———⟫·◦·⟪———

The truth is that you don't have to live in a quiet place to know the Infinite.

———⟫·◦·⟪———

Does experiencing the presence occur only in idyllic natural settings? Do you have to live in the midst of forest serenity? Not at all.

"But how can I experience that presence," you might ask, "if I live in a city that blares with traffic, with jackhammers that snarl and sirens that howl, with garbage trucks that clatter before dawn? Who has time for inner stillness when my baby's wailing for her bottle? I've got meals to cook, clients to please, a day-care schedule to balance."

The truth is that you don't have to live in a quiet place to know the Infinite. I've found myself in the presence in the most unlikely situations— during moments that looked anything but holy. I've experienced the presence in a confrontation with an angry friend yelling at me two and a half feet away. I was aware of it during a near accident when a tractor-trailer came within inches of sideswiping my Honda on a Tennessee interstate. I knew the Eternal was at hand late one night listening to folksingers on a Rhode Island beach, while sipping hot and sour soup in a Szechwan restaurant. I felt the presence during the boredom of forced small talk with guests at dinner and while munching on dry-roasted peanuts on a Delta jet awaiting takeoff in Dallas.

All these situations had something divine in them. Why? Not because of *me* or anything I did. Not because the situations were peaceful, but because grace allowed me to remember and acknowledge Eternity.

Life doesn't have to be gentle or full of love. We can experience the presence anywhere, anytime—even in confusion. Awareness of the presence can occur in unexpected situations, in barren, commercial settings where you'd least expect a glimpse to occur.

AN EMERGENCY AT A MALL

About a year ago, my wife, Kat, lost consciousness in a shopping mall. It happened on an easygoing Saturday morning after we'd driven the three hours from Ashland north to Eugene, in central Oregon. We'd just come out of a camping equipment store when Kat began to feel dizzy. As her legs buckled, I clutched her limp body, one arm encircling her waist. Somehow I dragged her thirty or so yards down a corridor until we reached a long oak bench. I placed her across the bench and rested her head in my lap.

At first, my mind was full of questions: "What's going on? Is something terrible happening to Kat?

Where do I find a doctor? How do I get her out of this mall? Do I need an ambulance? Damn it, I don't even know where there's a hospital!" Then I began to notice the presence of a deep stillness. Familiar with it, I knew that something beyond my fear of the moment was with us. In the midst of the commotion, I focused on the stillness.

⟫◦⟪

As I focused my awareness on the stillness, I silently acknowledged it. A realization that I didn't need to worry replaced my fears.

⟫◦⟪

In a few minutes security guards rushed over. Then two paramedics arrived. One of them, an athletic-looking woman dressed in khaki, gently questioned me:

"Any history of heart disease?"

"No."

"Any allergies?"

"None that I know of."

"Has she had anything to eat this morning?"

"A cup of coffee, a strawberry yogurt, and some trail mix in the car as we drove up."

As I answered her questions, I still sensed the presence. Moment by moment it reminded me that, no matter how the situation looked, in some way everything was unfolding perfectly, even if that moment seemed bleak, even as Kat lay gray and lifeless, draped over the bench. As I focused my awareness on the stillness, I silently acknowledged it. A realization that I didn't need to worry replaced my fears.

I looked down at Kat. Her face, though still dull and gray, showed more life. She returned my look and whispered a few words that let me know that she also experienced the presence.

The other paramedic, when he saw that Kat's blood pressure had plummeted, said, "We need to take her to the hospital." As I followed the ambulance in my car, the feeling of a deeper calm remained.

After an hour or so in the emergency room, Kat felt better. It turned out she was all right, and her severe reactions had been triggered by a recent bout with the flu. The episode passed, and we left the hospital together. Since then, the presence keeps reminding us that even in the thick of turmoil, we can turn to the Infinite.

THE PRESENCE AMID CHAOS

We can experience the presence in ugly situations, sometimes even in places where horror reigns. In the following excerpt, edited from his book *The Child Within Us Lives!*, William Samuel describes just such an incident he experienced as a young captain in the Korean War:

> My regiment was hit by an enormous wave of shellfire and oncoming Chinese troops. Hell erupted. In the early moments of that terrible onslaught everything that moved

was slaughtered ten times over—advancing troops, men, women, children, dogs, and chickens and every moving creature caught at that place at that time. I was suddenly unable to hear. My world went silent and I was enveloped in an immeasurable calm.

In the midst of that horrendous din of exploding bodies and shells, I could hear nothing but my own voice. In some marvelous way, I was caught up in a tranquil dimension, separate, but attached to the carnage at hand. . . . I could hear my own voice and even my breathing quite clearly. I went from gun position to gun position and heard myself giving calm encouragement to my troops. I could see their mouths move in reply and gratitude—and terror—but I couldn't hear them. I was beset with a wonderful enwrapping calm that let me move fearlessly to do whatever the moment asked me to do, as hideous as those moments were.

As the preceding stories illustrate, we can experience glimpses anywhere—on a dirt road in the southern Oregon mountains, in a suburban shopping mall, on a distant Korean battlefield. But simply knowing glimpses happen anywhere isn't enough.

Unless we recognize them as they take place, we miss their true meaning. They're really the Divine dropping in on us! They're Eternity greeting us, letting us know, "I'm here, within you, all around you. This is your chance to acknowledge me, to transcend your ordinary ways."

So the first step lies in recognizing glimpses. We need to know what to look for.

Chapter Four
RECOGNIZING GLIMPSES

As a ten-year-old living in northern Virginia, I sometimes stood in line on Saturday afternoons to see a double feature at the Fairfax theater. Once, as I watched a black-and-white Western, one of the bad guys who wore a black felt hat aimed his six-gun at the center of John Wayne's chest. "Stick 'em up," he snarled. And I, sitting there in the dark, with the smell of old popcorn and spilled Cokes, jerked both my arms up high. Magic and make believe were real then.

In *At the Sign of the Naked Waiter,* Amy Herrick describes the awe that a young girl feels as she walks to school: "The dogwood tree was in full bloom and

held its earnest white blossoms up to the sky like little plates . . . squirrels raced up and down fences and
birds shot through the air carrying twigs and string
and bits of old mattress ticking. Insects fizzed and
buzzed through the yellow veils of forsythia."
Childhood for her was full of wonder.

As children, we saw miracles all around us. We
delighted in fireflies and slobbering dogs. We felt in
awe of jets taxiing along an airport runway. But as
we grew older, our childlike enthusiasm waned. Not
wanting to seem naive, we learned sophistication.
Now, as adults, it's harder for us to recognize miracles. Unless something catches us off guard, like a
bold morning sun that bursts over a hillside or a
two-week-old golden retriever pup that nibbles on
our fingers, many of us have grown too worldly to
notice wonder. Suspicious of miracles, we dismiss
anything we cannot prove, including the Divine.

But in rejecting the Divine for lack of proof,
we miss something crucial. The proof exists! By
proof I don't mean research to delight an Old
Testament scholar or briefs to satisfy a brilliant legal
mind. It's far simpler than that. The proof lies in

glimpses that come from our own experience. These glimpses give us the evidence we need to know Eternity exists. They *are* the Divine as it appears in our everyday lives.

As children, we saw miracles all around us. We delighted in fireflies and slobbering dogs.

Not only are glimpses real but we can confirm them, again, by looking at what we experience. When we fall in love, do we doubt we're in love or do we know it? Do we need a Tibetan lama with lineage to validate it? Not at all. We know we're in love because we've *experienced* it. That's our proof! Does this sound too obvious? Too simple? It *is* that simple.

Just as when we fall in love, we need no proof of the presence of the Divine other than our own experience. When we're consciously aware of glimpses, that simple experience itself is proof we're in the presence.

How do we recognize glimpses? What are their characteristics? How do we distinguish them from a peak experience or an ordinary good time? The answers lie in what happens during a glimpse. When we experience a glimpse, we nearly always experience one or more of the following states of awareness.

THE INTELLECT RECEDES

The mind, eager to profess its own intelligence, loves to spew out knowledge. It thrives on caution, beliefs, judgments, and comparisons. With its instinct to thumb its nose at anything that can't be proven, the intellect obstructs glimpses of the presence. "Presence—what presence? That's wishful thinking!" For the mind, it's safer to remain skeptical than to be thought foolish.

No story better shows how the mind gets in the way of experiencing glimpses than the following fable. In his book *London Notes and Lectures*, Walter Lanyon tells about a lighthearted centipede who delighted in life until the day a cricket asked him, "How do you know which foot to put forward first?" This set the little centipede to thinking. He realized that he didn't know which foot came first. He thought so hard and became so puzzled by this that he forgot how to use his legs and never moved again. The story's premise—that the mind gets in the way of spontaneity—holds equally true for glimpses.

When it comes to experiencing glimpses, it's best not to know. Stephen Wolinsky, author of *The Tao of Chaos*, writes, "The key is to *be willing to not know* without placing judgments, evaluations, or significance as to what that means. . . . we simply have to be willing to *not know* and experience *not knowing.*" This mind-set of not knowing encourages glimpses.

Still, it's not easy to curtail the intellect. For example, as a writer, wrapped up in word finders and thesauri, submerged in style manuals and collections of quotations, I get lost in my mind's thoughts. John Bailey, proud owner of a 2,600-page dictionary, spends hours poring over picayune facts in Infotrak, *Books in Print,* and *Literary Market Place* at the library. But to experience glimpses I need to slow down my mind. Only when I stop churning out ideas do I become aware of the presence. That's when I begin to let my love out—when I let my mind rest enough to acknowledge the almost imperceptible miracles that unfold every day. That's where joy lives, the place where glimpses occur!

<hr>

When I allow the no-mind, intuitive part of me to show through, life becomes full of essence. And I awaken to the presence.

<hr>

In that place, scholar John, who navigates the spell checker on his outdated computer, who spends ten minutes scrutinizing entries in *Roget's* to find the most precise verb, is nowhere around. Only when I surrender the grammarian's logic, the critic's opinions, the judge's mind-set, do I light up with the light that lies within. That's when I feel in touch with creation, with life's energy flow. That's where love is! When I allow the no-mind, intuitive part of me to show through, life becomes full of essence. And I awaken to the presence.

CHILDLIKE INNOCENCE RETURNS

Watch toddlers, eyes wide, gurgling and laughing at a pond's edge as they see ducks dip their heads beneath the water, tail feathers pointing to the sky. Two-year-olds don't fear being thought naive. They're lost in the wonder of the moment. That's what happens during a glimpse: the worldly intellect gives way to childlike innocence. If we're afraid of being innocent, it's difficult to come into the presence. Innocence comes from *not* taking life's small events for granted, from finding magic everywhere. It comes from admitting that what we see is wondrous and sacred.

To experience glimpses, we need to let our innocence radiate. The skeptic who grumbles, "Don't be silly, it's no big deal!" keeps glimpses at bay. So do we when we bottle up our feelings and bury our spontaneity. We also end up stifling joy. Building ever more placid facades, we lose our childlike enthusiasm.

If we're afraid of being innocent,
it's difficult to come into the presence.

My father, a bald, stern-looking man with critical eyes and a small, grim mouth, never uttered the word *love*. He found it impossible to express feelings. Abandoned by his alcoholic father when he was only fourteen, he had to grow up quickly. His need to be responsible squelched his innocence.

On Thursday evenings my father enjoyed nothing more than watching *Perry Mason* on television.

Never taking his eyes off the screen, he'd watch the burly lawyer with fierce eyebrows pit his skills against Hamilton Berger, district attorney. Absorbed in guessing the murderer's identity week after week, he was the program's most devoted fan.

But if you asked him how he liked *Perry Mason*, he would only say, "Oh it's pretty good, I guess, if you've got nothing better to do." Then he'd mutter, "I can take it or leave it." He never could display enthusiasm. For him to show joy about anything was taboo. His innocence had shut down years ago.

There are a few who live among us who embody innocence. Though it's easy for the sophisticated to laugh at them as naive or dismiss them as immature, in their innocence lies wisdom. Around them joy and the secrets of reality swirl. I remember the antics of one of these crazy wise ones.

Years ago on a windy afternoon, five of us gathered to celebrate the birthday of a visitor from northern California. We stood in a thickly forested yard as the late-autumn sun warmed us. My friend, a sixty-year-old mystic, devotee of quantum physics and Taoist tall tales, gazed at a nearby wild persimmon tree with its leaves falling. Suddenly, he bounded off toward it, laughing and flailing his arms as he tried to catch a leaf—any leaf—before it landed. Yelping in delight, he pointed to me, shouting into the wind, "Come on John, catch a leaf, catch one if you can!"

⇒○⇐

To this fool belongs the innocence that nurtures bliss.

⇒○⇐

With both arms outstretched, I raced full-tilt into the eye of twirling leaves that spun and glided as they fell. But the leaves eluded me. Each one I grabbed for, I missed. Then, at the last second, the outstretched fingers of my right hand scooped one up, just as I and the leaf nearly hit the ground.

"You got one, you got one!" my friend shouted for the universe to hear. He didn't worry what others thought or that some might think him immature.

"You got one!" he continued to shout, as he kept up his primal dance. Some might see him and say, "What's the matter, can't he act his age? Why isn't he doing something productive, instead of acting like a fool?"

It's true, of course; he *is* a fool, a splendid fool, this lover of the Tao and trees, lover of cyberspace—and Eternity. Yes, he's a fool, a fool who's younger than some half his age who, with brilliant minds, toil at legal briefs and spreadsheets with self-adjusting bottom lines.

To this fool belongs the innocence that nurtures bliss.

❧

WE LIVE IN THE PRESENT

In her book *Everyday Zen*, spiritual teacher Charlotte Joko Beck underscores how the present influences spiritual life. "The only people who live comfortably," writes Beck, "are those who learn not to dream their lives away, but to be with what's right-here-now, no matter what it is: good, bad, nice, not nice, headache, being ill, being happy. It doesn't make any difference."

To experience glimpses, we need to live in the present. If our minds spin with past and future fantasies, it's impossible to notice the Infinite, even when it's right at hand.

Stop for a second. Right now as you look at these words, what's going on? Is it just that you're reading words in chapter 4? Allow your mind to slow down. At first it may feel uncomfortable to pay attention to this moment. What do you sense? What do you hear? Is there a gentle sound in the background that you've overlooked? Do you feel a vibration within your body? A subtle shift in your perception? Could the wonder of Eternity be present *right now?*

Our event-driven lives deter glimpses. When we're lost in our thoughts about the past and future, it's difficult to notice glimpses. We stride along a sidewalk wondering what we'll eat for dinner, ignoring what's happening around us. We miss the leaves that are beginning to bud. We shrug off the smile of a silver-haired woman who limps toward us.

She'd like to make eye contact, but we're asleep. We drive to work unconscious of the road we're driving on and the buildings we pass because we're already worried about what we'll say later to our boss.

To experience glimpses, we need to live in the present. If our minds spin with past and future fantasies, it's impossible to notice the Infinite, even when it's right at hand.

We all devise techniques to avoid living in the present. Yet now is the only place where glimpses appear. If we can't experience the present moment, glimpses won't reveal themselves to us. Do you recognize any of the following people, prone to avoiding what's happening now?

The Event-Driven, who spend most of their time anticipating or reminiscing about funerals and weddings, films and plays, baseball and football games—or the surgery on their gallstones.

The Vacation Enthusiasts, who show you countless slides and snapshots, proof they really did visit the Grand Tetons or the Colosseum.

The Good-Food Conversationalists, who recount the details of past meals ("This reminds me of that superb dinner I had one night in New Orleans") yet never actually taste the shrimp or okra in the gumbo they're having now.

The Conversation Robots, who, when asked how they're doing, reply, "fine," "great," or "never better," though if they stopped to tune in, they might respond, "Terrible. I've had a rotten day."

The Constant Talkers, who won't permit a conversational pause. Though they pretend they're listening, they're only waiting for their next chance to interrupt and tell you more about themselves.

The Moral High Grounders, who spend all their time debating politics, convinced there's an inherent right and wrong to every issue, and they, by no coincidence, always hold the former opinion.

What all these people share is a reluctance (sometimes even an unwillingness) to experience the present moment. Fortunately, it's easy to shift our perspective from the past and future to now—the only place where glimpses of the presence dwell.

------&-------

At that moment, there were no clocks or schedules, no worries about tomorrow. I sensed the presence of wonder.

------&-------

Sometimes it takes only a tiny moment to awaken us to the present. One clear subzero night, I drove home on a side road through heavily wooded countryside near Chanhassen, Minnesota. Suddenly, to the right in a clearing, I saw a deer with its nose pointing toward the moon. As I stopped the car, the doe turned her head and for a few seconds looked right at me. Then she scampered off into the woods. Moonlight bathed the tree branches. At that moment, there were no clocks or schedules, no worries about tomorrow. I sensed the presence of wonder. I felt carefree, full of the love of God: "Thank you for this special moment—this is *it!*"

OUR PERCEPTION CHANGES

During a glimpse we perceive events differently. We have a heightened sense of awareness. We're more likely to allow things to happen rather than to try to make them happen. Everything seems effortless.

Some people have a sensation of increased light. Others see objects as being more hazy than usual. Some sense a vibration within their chests or hear a background hum similar to the sound of *om*. Since these and other shifts in perception are subtle, we need to be still enough to detect their nuances.

———•—

With the witness perspective,
we acknowledge there's a reality
that transcends our normal way
of looking at things.

———•—

During glimpses we're often detached, looking on life as if we're observers instead of participants. Our wants and needs recede as the witness perspective replaces self-concern. This means that we don't lose ourselves in what's happening in our lives. We may still feel sad, glad, depressed, or even cantankerous. But we're not immersed in the feelings. It's as if for a while we're watching a play, even if the play is about ourselves.

With the witness perspective, we acknowledge there's a reality that transcends our normal way of looking at things. It's as if we can imagine there's a witness—God, the universe, nature, or consciousness—that looks through our eyes, watching everything without opinions or judgments.

Adopting this perspective doesn't mean we're befuddled mystics or that we're lost in spiritual pipe dreams. We can still floss our teeth, cast a vote for the politician we support, scour the bathtub with Comet, or grab a take-out dinner of fried rice and Kung Pao chicken. We can do all these things, acting responsibly in the world, and *still* grasp that there's a divine scene unfolding all around us.

Once we know how to recognize glimpses, there's one more important step: to *acknowledge* glimpses. We admit, "Yes, there is something special happening right now, something wondrous that's beyond me, beyond all I can see, touch, and feel. That something is the presence making itself known." What we're doing is acknowledging that something greater than us transcends the scene at hand.

Without this acknowledgment of something beyond, the glimpse is incomplete—another moment of joy that passes by. We need to affirm the glimpse is *not* a coincidence. Nor is it due to anything we've done. We acknowledge instead that Eternity is its sole source.

"At the heart of every event in this world," says European teacher Karlfried Graf Dürckheim, "we can be touched by a reality that has nothing to do with the world: it is another dimension that transcends the usual horizon of our consciousness."

Though the transcendent reality Dürckheim describes isn't worldly, we can perceive it with our senses. But this isn't the ordinary seeing and hearing we're used to. Effortlessness and letting go characterize this way of perceiving things. So does paradox. We see but don't use our eyes in old ways that draw distinctions. We listen, but the sound we hear is soundless.

❦

Chapter Five
NOTICING THE SOUNDLESS SOUND

Grace comes to us in countless ways. No one way is best or more spiritual; no one way more evolved. You may sense a glimpse of the presence as a vibration in your body or as a feeling of stillness and well-being. Perhaps you see objects around you in a haze of pale yellow. Or you're simply aware of a few moments of transcendent calm. The clues that reveal the presence differ for each of us. For me and for others I've known, it often comes as what some call "the soundless sound."

When I was fifteen and had a room of my own upstairs from my parents, I'd lie in bed reading spy novels late into the night. Then I'd put on my clock radio and turn the volume down. I'd listen to the sounds of Fats Domino and Little Richard, the Drifters and the Midnighters, beamed in from rhythm-and-blues stations in Memphis and Buffalo.

Some nights after I turned the radio off, I'd hear a mysterious sound whose low pitch kept me awake. I'd turn my head on the pillow, first to one side, then the other, trying to get rid of the sound. "Am I hearing things?" I'd worry. "Maybe I've got an ear infection." Wanting to forget the sound, I dismissed the pesky intruder. I didn't realize then what this sound had to teach me, or that some people looked on it as sacred. "Listen to the secret sound, the real sound, which is inside you," advises the fifteenth-century Indian and Sufi poet Kabir, in these lines translated by Robert Bly. "The one no one talks of speaks the secret sound to himself, and he is the one who has made it all."

Years later, when I lived in New York City, I never thought about that mysterious sound. Caught up in starting a career in marketing, in building new relationships, in absorbing the intensity and allure

of living in Manhattan, I had no use for a sound I'd
never understood.

---

*As I meditated more and my life
quieted, something else happened.
The sound that I hadn't heard for
more than ten years returned.*

Then in my late twenties I began to meditate.
Twice a day, I sat on a thick brown cushion and
repeated my transcendental meditation mantra. My
life began to quiet down. Until then, I'd needed to
fill every waking moment with *doing* things. I lis-
tened to the music of the Stones, Joni Mitchell, Van
Morrison, and Jerry Jeff Walker. I saw off-Broadway
plays, read *Rolling Stone* and *The New York Times*. I
drank pints of draft beer and smoked fat Jamaican
joints at West Side parties that rocked into the

dawn. But when I started to meditate, my need for excitement diminished.

As I meditated more and my life quieted, something else happened. The sound that I hadn't heard for more than ten years returned. I'd read passages from Nisargadatta Maharaj's book *I Am That*, and I'd hear the sound. I'd listen to a gifted psychotherapist speak about spiritual awakening, and as he spoke his first words, the sound would fill my ears, continuing its hum until he finished his talk. Each time I heard the sound, a sense of calm accompanied it. Everything around me would seem especially serene.

One spring, I visited a film actor who had a small apartment on De La Vina Street in Santa Barbara. Long before we met, I knew from his letters that he was a fervent God-lover. As I sat in a green vinyl chair in my air-conditioned room at the Best Western a few blocks from his studio apartment, the sound began to hum. I started to suspect that the sound that disturbed me as a teenager echoed the rhythm of the universe, bringing with it awareness of the presence.

How do we hear the soundless sound? What does it sound like?

Remember a time at the beach when you held a seashell up to your ear. Didn't it sound like the soft murmur of the sea? The soundless sound is like that. It seems to fill your ears with sound, yet you can't pinpoint its origin. Neither loud nor dramatic, it's more likely to be heard as a whisper than a roar. Sometimes it vibrates at a high pitch. At other times it sounds like the wind whistling far away. Or you may only hear a faint hiss. Salim Michaël, the British author of *The Way of Inner Vigilance*, describes it as a "crystal-like vibration which resembles the noise of the ocean with many other different 'ultra' sounds superimposed on it."

While the soundless sound often arrives in quiet places when we're silent, it can also arrive amid noise that clamors. I've heard it above the car radio while barreling south on Interstate 5 to Bakersfield, California, from the Bay Area. I've also heard it in our living room near Minneapolis as Northwest Airlines jets swoop over our house on their path to the airport.

You won't, of course, find much evidence to corroborate the soundless sound. No Sony tape recorder can detect its vibration. No sound machine can measure its decibels. Yet once you hear it and grasp its meaning, you realize beyond doubt that this nearly imperceptible sound represents oneness.

"If we will but trust that little voice, its tones will become plainer and stronger, and we will hear it on many occasions," writes turn-of-the-century philosopher Yogi Ramacharaka. Then he adds a note of caution: "If we turn a deaf ear to it and refuse to heed its warning and guidance, it will gradually grow fainter and fainter, until its voice is no longer distinguishable amid the roar and bustle of the material world."

The soundless sound, like the glimpses described in earlier chapters, reminds us of our Eternal essence. It tells us that here, in a world of pain and violence, we can know the presence that endures beyond it all. It, like glimpses, suggests we can put our attention on it instead of on suffering and confusion.

It's not easy to describe the soundless sound. "It is something to be experienced, not explained," says Gyomay Kubose, founder of Chicago's Buddhist Temple. "Each person can hear the soundless sound. . . . It is unique yet universal. Find it. Listen to it. Live it."

———⇒»-๐-«⇐———

Never judging, never sermonizing,
the soundless sound arrives,
confirming the presence of perfection.
The potential to hear it is
always present.

———⇒»-๐-«⇐———

In recent years, I've begun to value the sound. It, in turn, has shown me new ways of being. It often shows up when I'm least self-concerned—when I'm most detached from the present moment. Paradoxically, the soundless sound sometimes arrives when I'm selfish, full of what I want. When

I'm angry with my next-door neighbor, who has just complained about the dandelions covering my lawn, the sound arrives and seems to whisper, "Here I am. You can choose to stay with your ego's anger or you can turn to love." As I notice this choice, anger and self-righteousness fade.

Never judging, never sermonizing, the soundless sound arrives, confirming the presence of perfection. The potential to hear it is always present. "The sound of Being resonates all the time," writes Karlfried Graf Dürckheim in *Dialogue on the Path of Initiation.* "We must learn how to hear this sound. The opportunity of having such an experience is here at every instant." That doesn't mean we can always hear it. Some may not hear it or may feel inclined to dismiss it. Others may hear it, yet never attribute special meaning to it.

If we're sensitive to its call, however, the soundless sound tells us the Infinite is here with us. It, like the other clues that announce the presence, shows us how to transcend the fears and desires of our self-centered egos and experience awareness of God.

PART TWO
OUR OBSESSION WITH ME

*The selfish ego
can lead us
into the presence.*

Chapter Six
THE ME-SENSE

Inside each of us lurks a creature who controls our every move. We know this cunning beast by various names. The Bible calls it "the old man" or human self. Eastern sages call it "the ego." Don't mistake this ego, however, for the ego who reclines on couches of Freudian psychoanalysts. This ego is no dignified manager of the personality.

This ego—crass and bullheaded—clings to cars and money; it covets good-tasting food and titillating sex. This ego bristles at insults and demands that people fawn over it. It lusts and craves, judges, rants, and raves. If you watch it for more than a minute or two, you'll notice how it bickers and complains, becomes downcast and disturbed. When out of sorts, it joins in concert with other egos to wipe out forests and launch barbaric wars. From time to time, it also excels at helping us learn new ways to fear and hate.

———»-o-«———

Most of us don't realize how me dominates our lives. We take our self-centeredness for granted.

———»-o-«———

In his book *Awakening from the Dream of Me*, David Manners calls the ego-critter the "me-sense." "How easy it is to get involved with the mind and its concern with money, clothes, friends, likes and dislikes!" he writes. "All these trifles go on while consciousness is present. We constantly ignore the wonder we are, settling for dust, rather than the real wealth that is ours." Manners continues, "Only when the me-person is absent can wholeness be realized."

Most of us don't realize how *me* dominates our lives. We take our self-centeredness for granted. For a long time I believed *others,* such as actors, politicians, and business tycoons, had big egos. I didn't admit how much my own life revolved around John Bailey.

For years everything I thought about centered on *me: my* wife, *my* backache, *my* unfair boss, *my* writing, *my* car—even *my* gifts to charity. At some point I realized that with the exception of Kat, the woman I love, John Bailey was the basis for how I lived. The first step in becoming aware of my ego was to finally admit how much the me-sense controlled my thoughts.

At first, as I turned my attention minutely on John Bailey, my me-focus intensified. My ego ballooned. No matter what I did or where I went, I couldn't get away from *me. Me* popped up everywhere. I felt like a walking egomaniac!

Then something extraordinary happened. During the times I was most full of myself, I became aware that something else existed—something beyond me. It was as if an unspoken voice within urged me to notice all this focus on me—and then to put my awareness elsewhere. I consciously switched my focus from me to that which is vaster than me, that which is all-encompassing. The same me-thoughts that I'd seen as selfish began to help me remember the Divine. Why did I begin to remember? I suspect it was due to wanting to get beyond my egotistical perspective.

During the times I was most full of myself, I became aware that something else existed— something beyond me.

What a paradox! I saw that whenever I was wrapped up in myself, I could use that self-concern to come into the presence of Eternity. The obsession with *me* could remind me of the Infinite!

When we use the ego in this way, we no longer have to think of ourselves as unspiritual and selfish when we're full of ourselves. The selfishness itself becomes yet another teacher who helps us awaken.

ME DEFINED

Exactly who is this *me* that obsesses us so?

The ego is the part of us that incessantly looks out for what *I* want, what *I* need, what *I* think *I* must have. The ego is the uncertain one who worries about the future. It is our insecure, fearful side that holds grudges and feels shy, annoyed, or left out. *Me* emerges when we're indignant, convinced the world should treat us better.

The same sense of *me* looms if I feel furious when a driver beside me speeds up, then swerves in front of my car, forcing me to slam on the brakes. *Me* erupts when I call him a jerk. *Me* surfaces in the supermarket checkout line if I glower at a woman in a mink coat when she butts ahead in line. *Me* lurks when I judge her as insensitive, a killer of small animals. *Me* is in control when I'm addicted to garlic, chocolate, computer software, or what people think about me.

The me-sense comments on *everything*—including me. An overblown me-sense makes me believe I'm important. *Me* wants to buy the new Japanese car I saw in the latest issue of *Motor Trend*. *Me* worries that people at the party thought I was a bore. *Me* constantly looks for something new to eat or buy. *Me* thinks I'm entitled to a quick response to the letter I just sent. *Me* eats organic broccoli and oat bran so that I'll live longer. *Me* believes I'm too intense, not outgoing enough, too interested in *me*. This sense of *me* spawns countless thoughts, encouraging us to believe that our needs and desires are critical, that our perceptions count. For some of us, *me* is the only reality that matters.

In the spiritual realm, too, *me* likes to take charge. *Me* doesn't accept God's absence. *Me* wants God at my beck and call. *Me* desires spiritual progress, transcendent experiences, and enlightenment. *Me* wants experiences of oneness to last. *Me* would like me to be more loving and gentle. *Me* wants me to be unattached and desireless—regardless of how I am. *Me* never says, "Thy will be done," and *means* it. It's the me-sense's inherent nature to control things, to avoid surrender, to ignore the Divine.

━━━➤●◄━━━

> *But the John Bailey who owns things will die. So will Kat. And one day our house will crumble or get torn down. Indeed, nothing we can see or touch endures. The only thing that lasts is the Infinite.*

━━━➤●◄━━━

The me-sense entrenches itself in most of us and becomes the basis for how we live. Even when we think of others, our thoughts frequently revert back to *me:*

- "*I* love her so—she makes *me* feel happy."
- "I'm glad *I* gave to Greenpeace this year."

- "Wonder if they got the Christmas present *I* sent them?"
- "If she dies, how can *I* live without her?"

As negative as it seems, there's really nothing wrong with all this me-emphasis. It's simply the orientation we grow up with—one of countless defense mechanisms that help us survive. It may not occur to us that our real identity lies with the Infinite. We all go through a stage where we believe this sense of me is who we really are. Sometimes I hear myself say, "*I'm* a writer." "This is *my* wife, Kat." Or, "We've lived in *our* house for three years."

But the John Bailey who owns things will die. So will Kat. And one day our house will crumble or get torn down. Indeed, nothing we can see or touch endures. The only thing that lasts is the Infinite. Why identify with what perishes when we can identify with Eternity. The problem lies in transcending the me-sense. How do we get beyond ourselves and identify with that which lasts? Oddly enough, the very me-sense we're obsessed with can awaken us to the Divine.

❦

Chapter Seven
LOOSENING THE EGO'S GRIP

Like the radar that whirls above the deck of a guided missile cruiser, we constantly scan our environment, evaluating how everything affects us. In one way or another, we perpetually ask, "What does this mean for me?"

It's rare, for example, that any of us spends more than a minute or two without our thoughts reverting back to *me*. Few among us would dispute that we care deeply about ourselves. Yet the great sages point out that this same ego is the arch enemy who blocks our way to awakening. The personality, they tell us, stifles our connection with the Infinite. Our desires and selfishness—our ceaseless concern with ourselves—block our spiritual development.

Shankara, the brilliant twelfth-century Vedanta philosopher, condemned the me-sense: "The ego is a strong and deadly serpent." Then he warned that as long as we identify ourselves with "this wicked ego, there can be no possibility of liberation. For liberation is its very opposite."

When we first discover how the ego controls us, we're likely to feel uneasy. How can we love Eternity and yet be so obsessed with ourselves? As we begin to recognize the ego as our enemy, curtailing its influence becomes the goal of spiritual practice. Yet the act of trying to overcome the ego is directed by none other than the ego itself!

What then can we do about this puffed-up ego that preoccupies us so? Some spiritual paths suggest numbing the mind by fasting, chanting, repeating mantras, or asking ourselves *koans*. Still others advise poring over the wisdom of the Bible, the *Baghavad Gita*, or the *Tao Te Ching*. Or they suggest we study with an enlightened teacher.

But no matter what we do, the ego persists. The more we try to loosen its hold, the more it clings. Trying to empty our minds of all thoughts only reinforces the mistaken idea that *me*—rather than Eternity—controls what happens. We may become proficient meditators or obedient disciples of a guru, yet in themselves these efforts don't diminish the ego's clout. Trying to dismantle the ego only entrenches it.

❧

THE EGO'S AGENDA

Hell-bent pursuit of *me* without regard to consequences sooner or later brings consequences. Note that the word is *consequences,* not *God's punishment* or *wrath.* Though some believe the Bible depicts an angry God who torments us, there is no judgment from God that I've experienced.

The inflated ego isn't wrong or evil. It's a natural part of being imperfect, of being human. The ego's main shortcoming is that it obstructs our connection with the Infinite. When I focus on what *I* want and need, there's little room for much else. When I'm full of myself, I'm unaware of the gentle presence.

When we relentlessly pursue the me-agenda, the results we experience are due to cause and effect, not to immorality. Consume too many New York steaks or snort too much cocaine and we soon learn the drawbacks of pursuing *me*. The same is true if we chase after power, money, luxury cars, or anonymous sex. Cancer, bankruptcy, heart attacks, and sexually transmitted diseases are a few such teachers. There are, however, no divine judgments. The judgments, if they exist, come from ourselves or others—not from a sky-based God.

━━▶◦◀━━

Sooner or later most of us discover that a life based on desire is hollow.

━━▶◦◀━━

The shortcomings of this me-orientation are clear. When we pursue pleasure, the pleasure never lasts. The *risotto alla Milanese* dinner that we savor or the standup comedian's joke that makes us howl last only so long. So, too, does the spectacular sunset. In a few minutes or hours the experience ends. Though we may not want to admit it, this is always true.

If our goal is to experience joy, we ultimately fail, since the joy cannot last. So we search for one new stimulus after another, seldom content to simply *be*. Meanwhile, the temporary nature of the ego's pursuits leaves us unfulfilled. Sooner or later most of us discover that a life based on desire is hollow. Disappointment inevitably follows a stream of short-lived satisfactions. There's nothing wrong, of course, with pursuing the *me* desires. Nevertheless, the constant quest for our next injection of happiness is unsettling. Real joy—lasting joy—eludes us.

In the long run, all this emphasis on *me* is a good thing. It forces us to change. Once we experience the emptiness of a life based solely on wants and needs, the pain we feel eventually prompts us to ask, "Is this all there is? Isn't there something more to life?" The answers to these questions point to living from a sense of joy that comes only from looking to Eternity.

Yet the truth is that if most of the time life treats us well, those questions rarely occur to us.

The result? Most of us don't give the ego much thought. Usually it takes gut-wrenching pain for us to understand the drawbacks of a life centered on *me*. Not until we've suffered intensely do we suspect the vise-like grip of the me-sense. Many people go through their entire lives never questioning the role of *me*. Not surprisingly, it's the infantry private in the midst of combat or the humiliated husband or wife whose second marriage has just crumbled who may begin to question and look beyond.

THE EGO AS FRIEND

Once we realize the ego's limitations, what do we do with the anger, judgments, and self-obsessed thoughts that make up the me-sense? How do we deal with this self-concern that obstructs our connection with Eternity? What do we *do* with this attachment to everything that happens to *me?* Do we ignore the ego? Do we meditate or practice yoga? Do we isolate ourselves in an ashram or escape to a mountain cabin?

To be sure, we can always temporarily reduce the ego's influence by withdrawing to a secluded room where we recite endless mantras. Or we can go live in a spiritual community where everyone shares the same beliefs. The ego *will* recede. But if we rely only on the route of the recluse, what happens when we stop meditating? What happens when we get away from that serenity? Don't the ego's antics erupt once again as soon as we face the real world?

———❦———

There's another way to approach the ego that neither vilifies nor worships it—to embrace the ego as teacher.

———❦———

Diligently attempting to get rid of the ego inevitably fails. Trying hard only gives importance to the one who tries—the doer. But who is the doer? None other than the ego!

There's another way to approach the ego that neither vilifies nor worships it—to embrace the ego as teacher. The ego itself becomes the instrument that shows us how preoccupation with *me* runs our lives. Unless we realize how completely the ego dominates us, it's foolish to think about reducing its clout. Acknowledging our obsession with ourselves is the first step toward moving beyond the ego's dominance.

Using this approach, we no longer attempt to control the ego. Surrender takes the place of doing. We give up repeating exotic syllables and mantras. We stop running from one teacher to another looking for answers from human beings. We stop trying to be egoless and spiritually evolved. Instead we accept ourselves as we are. We do this, not with New Age affirmations that convince us we're already perfect, but by letting ourselves *be*.

Now we're ready to notice the ego. This means that we simply watch the me-entity, without judgments. This, too, is doing, but it's a quiet, inactive doing. How do we notice *me?* Where can we find *me?* What does *me* look like? The best way to get to know the ego is to watch it in action. We listen as the ego chatters. We watch how *me,* in the guise of what we want and feel, comments on everything: "I don't like Alice. . . . I want a new video recorder. . . . I hate short-sleeved polyester shirts. . . . I'm afraid my son uses cocaine. . . . If only I could have better sex. . . . I don't care for Republicans. . . . I'm worried about getting cancer. . . . I'm anxious about the bills piling up. . . . I'm scared of being left alone one day."

Instead of ignoring the ego, we look for it where it's most conspicuous. Anything that makes us suffer is a good place to spot the inflated ego. Addiction, workaholism, and compulsive sexuality are instances where the overblown me-sense cautions us, "Here I am—take a look at how I affect your life!"

Next, we experience the ego, without judgment, in the present. When we intentionally experience the me-sense, we discover the ego isn't as formidable as we thought.

How do we experience the ego? By going right into the feelings that originate in the me-sense— anger, fears, desires, and judgments—as they arise. But in working with these feelings, instead of expressing them to others, we quietly experience them.

For example, when we get a form letter telling us we didn't get the job we applied for, the disappointment we feel right then is the upset ego! Instead of ignoring the rejection, we can experience it fully! We silently acknowledge to ourselves, "*Me* is in control now. Yes, I'm hurt by what's happening to *me* right now. I want things my way." We accept the me-sense, honest and raw as it seems.

Thus we consciously feel what it's like to be afraid, angry, or anxious at the moments those feelings seem to control us. Instead of shunning them, we ask, "What am I feeling now?"

Once we've experienced the ego in this way, we're ready for perspective. Perspective means acknowledging that there's something going on beyond the immediate feelings. We let ourselves become aware of the Infinite's presence. We're aware the Eternal is with us. Now our focus shifts from merely experiencing feelings to looking beyond.

Something magical has happened. The selfish ego has helped us come into the presence!

❦

Chapter Eight
OVERCOMING JUDGMENTS

One cloudless Sunday morning I hiked with two friends along a dirt road in the foothills of southern Oregon's Siskiyou mountains. We were so preoccupied with calling the summer day "beautiful," the scenery "great," and the mountains "incredible" that we ignored the present moment. We were like film critics on a hike. But instead of reviewing a film, we offered our "thumbs up" on the forested mountains. With our minds full of judgments (albeit positive judgments), we focused our conversation on *describing* our experience. Meanwhile, we were *aware* of practically nothing.

Once I realized how lost I was in judging, I turned inward. At that moment, my awareness shifted. I saw a salamander dart across the road. I watched a deer, still and gaunt, standing at the edge of a clearing twenty or thirty yards away. I heard the "kaw" of an unseen crow at the top of an old pine tree.

⇒·◦·⇐

Too often our opinions dominate our thoughts, leaving little time to breathe in the smell of a damp tree after an overnight rain.

⇒·◦·⇐

When we judge, we miss these gifts. We miss not only the call of a bird, but joy, love, and the essence of the universe, which has its own soundless sound. Too often our opinions dominate our thoughts, leaving little time to breathe in the smell of a damp tree after an overnight rain. Or to experience a glimpse of grace when we're alone.

As human beings, it's natural for us to judge. We do it all the time. We judge with positive as well as negative labels. We judge as much with our *goods, brilliants,* and *successfuls* as with our *rottens, awfuls,* and *terribles.* Though at first the positive labels look harmless, they limit our experience. When I call my writing "compelling," it's not long before I label it "dull." The art critic who proclaims, "That's a good painting," soon says another is "bad." Judgments, even when they're positive, inevitably produce more judgments.

When we're judgmental, we overlook our immediate experience. Issuing our labels, we proclaim what's *right* and *wrong,* what's *better* and *worse,* what's *brilliant* and *stupid.* At the very moment we call the weather "rotten," we miss the magic of snow crystals that glisten after a December snowstorm. When we say, "You're such a good kitten," we might ignore the soft, fuzzy feel of the kitten's belly as it's stretched out at our feet. Our opinions turn us into clever commentators. But in the process of constantly evaluating everything, we're less conscious of life, less aware of the Eternal.

To be sure, we have good reasons for judging. Growing up, judgments taught us how to survive. As toddlers we learned cars were *dangerous* and that it was *bad* to poke the child next door in the eye. We also learned to discriminate, to distinguish friend from foe. Those lessons served us well. The labels taught us to be cautious around hot stoves and below-zero temperatures.

Another reason we judge is that judgments make it easy for us to summarize our experience: "Did you read her new novel?" "Yes, it was *boring*." Or "It was a *great* meal." Or "My patient is *narcissistic* and *passive-aggressive*." We don't have to describe every detail of the plot of *Citizen Kane* when we can exclaim, "What a *stunning* film!" We can dispense with telling friends about our trip to Seattle where it rained every day by saying, "It was a *lousy* vacation."

When we judge, labels replace our awareness of what's going on now. Layers of categories define our reality. "My friends are *open-minded*." "Those people down the street are *rednecks*." "The congresswoman is a *hypocrite*." "His New Age ideas are *flaky*."

Not even nature is immune from our judgments. We comment on today's *depressing* rain, that *ugly* elm, the *vicious* Doberman, or yesterday's *spectacular* sunset. But the rain is just being rain perfectly. Similarly, the elm, the Doberman, and the sunset are being themselves perfectly.

THE PRICE OF JUDGING

What's wrong with judging? Aren't judgments natural? If we didn't judge, how could we get along in the world? If we don't view alcohol as *harmful* or see that piling up debts is *risky*, wouldn't our lives be a mess? Isn't it critical to know what's *good* and *bad* for us? "Some people believe that if we let go of our constant judgmental overseer," writes author-teacher Stephen Levine in *A Gradual Awakening*, "we'll become wild, rabid beasts."

The problem with judgments is not so much that we judge, but that we judge so rampantly. Like dandelions on a hillside, our judgments abound. As labels and categories replace our experience, they leave little room for being. Our self-importance as commentators expands. But all the while we pay the price: Our spiritual aliveness diminishes.

Judgments prompt us to *view* life instead of *experience* it. We create separation between ourselves and what we judge. Like drama critics observing from the back row, we offer our opinions rather than being in the production and saying our lines.

———⟫•⟪———

As labels and categories replace our experience, they leave little room for being.

———⟫•⟪———

Once, on a misty spring morning in Minnesota, I said, "That lake looks surreal and beautiful." But as soon as I uttered the words, the experience left me and the lake seemed separate. When I judge, in effect I say, "Here I am, distant from everything around me." Similarly, the other evening during dinner, I said to Kat, "Aren't we having a great time!" The instant I described it, the feeling of joy disappeared. Judgments are like that. They remove us from what we experience.

Letting go of our judgments helps us reclaim our natural tendency to love. When judgments dominate, love lessens and caution comes to the fore. How much love can I feel for John Bailey, for others, or for God when I label my writing *trite,* the cloudy day *bleak,* and the car salesperson *slick?* How can I feel connected to others if I see them as better or worse than me? Watch how joy evaporates when a judgmental person walks into a room. It's difficult to feel content when you hear someone say the following:

- "I look *terrible* today."
- "Their marriage *failed.*"
- "His friend is an *unsuccessful* actor."
- "Can't you do a *decent* job of making the kids behave?"

Such labels deplete our energy. They snuff out joy. Recall what it's like to work for a fault-finding boss, someone who evaluates your every move. How do you respond around a relative who constantly judges you? How do you feel when you judge yourself *stupid* or *uncreative?* Doesn't your self-esteem wither?

As we remember to judge less, love blossoms in our lives. I remember one January evening in Minnetonka, Minnesota, when the temperature plunged to thirty degrees below zero. I drove into the parking lot of a SuperAmerica station and pulled up next to an old gray van. Its owner, a brawny man with a full red beard, swore as he bent over the van's right front tire. My first instinct was to judge him: "I won't help him. He looks *surly* and *mean.* Besides, if I try to help, I might end up looking *stupid.*"

But then another voice, nearly imperceptible, said, "Go ahead and offer. He's in trouble and needs help." "Do you need a jack?" I asked him. Immediately his expression changed. "Thanks," he said with a grin. "I appreciate it." At that moment, I was grateful I'd stopped judging.

Only when we notice our judgments and consciously experience them do we begin to judge less. Judgments close us off to the flow of life. Engrossed in our opinions, our self-importance balloons and our spontaneity shrivels. Over time we lose our innocence. What starts as a harmless judgment or two burgeons into a life bloated with judgments which impede our connection with the Divine.

LETTING GO OF OUR JUDGMENTS

Once we realize how judgments harm us, what do we do with them? How do we handle this urge to categorize everything?

We can take several steps to reduce our judgments. The first is to observe how much we judge. "The best means of defusing the judging mind," writes Levine, "is simply to nonjudgmentally recognize it as it occurs." This isn't easy at first because most of us take our judgments for granted. We can begin by looking for situations where our judgments proliferate. Judgments flourish, for example, when we feel bored or irritated. I've often watched my judgments come up while waiting in line for a teller at a bank.

"Why do I always have the bad luck to get the *slow* teller!"

"Look at the *pompous* loan officer in his dark gray flannel suit."

⟫•⟪

The more we watch our judgments without being hard on ourselves, the less likely they are to control us.

⟫•⟪

Once we recognize our judgments, we're ready for the second step: to accept ourselves for being judgmental. When we start noticing our judgments, we might think we're *bad* for judging. I've occasionally told myself, "There you go again being a judgmental jerk." But the worst thing we can do is judge ourselves for judging.

Then we take a third step. Rather than force ourselves to stop judging, we give ourselves permission to judge as much as we like! But instead of being lost in our judgments, we continue observing them. The more we watch our judgments without being hard on ourselves, the less likely they are to control us. At this point the judgments lessen. Then, we turn our attention to the Eternal. This shift, more than anything else, decreases our judgments—and helps us recognize the presence.

Chapter Nine
WHO AM I?

As natural as they are, our judgments and obsession with *me* create a barrier in spiritual life: the hyperactive mind. How do we calm this capricious rascal who has an opinion on everything? With a mind that constantly chatters with judgments, with fears and desires kindled by the ego, it's impossible to hear Eternity's whisper.

The answer lies in meditation. If we can curtail the mind's ramblings, then the power of the me-sense will diminish. Only when we've reduced the me-sense's influence can we begin to shift our focus from the ego to Eternity.

❧

MEDITATION

Meditation's structure quiets the mind. By concentrating on a syllable or on how we breathe, we reduce the barrage of thoughts that assault us. As we repeat a mantra or count our exhalations, the mind becomes one-pointed. Over time we're less likely to get lost in every emotion, every fleeting idea.

Taming the restless mind isn't easy. Our brain, used to running untethered, abhors restraint. Thoughts, opinions, fantasies, and impatience intrude. The mind doesn't want to slow down!

Twenty years ago, when I began meditating, my judgments often got in the way. As I sat in a half-lotus on the floor of my apartment in Manhattan, I worried I wasn't meditating well. "What a terrible meditation! All I did was think about the news. Why can't I have good meditations like Karen?" Or I'd tell myself, "That was a great meditation," as if meditations could be inherently good or bad. I put all my effort into meditating correctly. But in the process of meditating diligently, I was rarely conscious of the Infinite.

———⟫•⟪———

The biggest problem with meditation arises when we believe meditating in itself is important, that the activity of meditating is somehow sacred.

———⟫•⟪———

Sometimes meditating made me feel important. During one period I believed I was more spiritual than the people I knew who didn't meditate. My ego expanded. I often heard other meditators display a similar sense of superiority when they talked about their meditations:

"I felt a bolt of energy move into my heart *chakra*."

"There was a lot of light in my meditation and I saw the blue pearl."

"I felt I *was* the universe."

Meditation, a technique originally meant to bring us closer to God, had become just another accomplishment to brag about.

The biggest problem with meditation arises when we believe meditating in itself is important, that the activity of meditating is somehow sacred. When this happens, we're focused on the ritual. We forget that it's the Infinite that's worthy of our attention—not some yogic technique devised by human beings.

CONTEMPLATION: WHO AM I?

Ramana Maharshi, one of modern India's great spiritual teachers, advocated a simple practice that he viewed as the most direct path to God. He called it self-inquiry or *vichara*. Instead of trying to get rid of our thoughts by structured breathing techniques and mantra repetition, Maharshi suggested that we turn within and ask ourselves, "Who Am I? Just who is it that's having this thought about . . . ?" This investigation of the self lies at the core of his teachings.

The sage himself describes self-inquiry in these words: "When other thoughts arise, one should not pursue them, but should inquire: 'To whom did they arise?' The answer that would emerge would be 'To me.' Thereupon if one inquires 'Who am I?' the mind will go back to its source."

The cause of our suffering, explains Maharshi, is that we identify ourselves with the body. Our constant I-thoughts illustrate this misidentification. We can alter this belief by inquiring deeply into the origin of *I*. How does *I* come about? From where does the I-thought come? As other thoughts arise, we ask, "To whom is this thought arising?"

We're not sure what to expect when we ask, "Who am I?" The question may seem pointless at first. The mind instinctively wants to answer with a ready phrase such as, "I am love," or "I am God." But the object isn't to respond with words. If we look for an answer at all, it's an answer removed from logic, removed from the realm of the senses. Wordless, it lies beyond description.

When I used to repeat my mantra hundreds of times, I often succeeded in making my mind nearly blank. But I didn't feel closer to the presence. Meditation then seemed like a spiritual formula that tranquilized my brain but didn't do much for my soul.

——➤◦◄——

In asking "Who am I?" it's best if
we allow ourselves to be quiet, to
simply be with our experience.

——➤◦◄——

During the times I became dissatisfied with meditation as a technique, I found I could go deeper into the self by asking myself Maharshi's question "Who am I?" But I had to be careful. Sometimes I turned even this simple question into a meaningless ritual.

Years ago I tore the ligament of my left knee running up a steep mountain path. Worried the pain might persist for years and that I'd never run again, my thoughts made it hard to be in the presence.

By meditating on "Who am I?" I learned to shift my focus from my aches and pains to the presence. After asking each "Who am I" question, I'd pause for a few seconds or so and let myself be still.

Who is the one who listens? Who hears the tractor-trailers in the distance roar by on Interstate 5? Who is the one who wonders if asking this question is a waste of time? Who's fed up with sitting here like a robot? Who feels like he's not accomplishing anything? Who wants to get on with my day? Am I the one who asks?

Am I the body that feels allergic to the pollen outside? Am I the body that runs in the late afternoon? Who is the *me* that just injured himself running? Who is the *me* that gets in a foul mood when his knee throbs as he limps down the basement steps? Who can't bear the thought he might not run again?

Who is the one who feels dissatisfied? Who is this person with a body and a brain and feelings that change? Am I the one who one day gets buried in the earth, where worms, insects, and tree roots will feed on what's left of me? Am I the one who has a sister who lives on Long Island and parents from Texas and Virginia who died years ago?

Who is this person who writes books? Who am I when I get beyond my name, my job, the woman I'm married to, my ancestors, and the country I live in? Who am I when I sense I'm none of these things? Who is aware that I'm asking these questions? Who watches my thoughts? Who sees through these eyes when my thoughts are absent? Who really asks? Who am I?

In asking "Who am I?" it's best if we allow ourselves to be quiet, to simply *be* with our experience.

There's no need to accomplish anything. We're passive. Our attitude is one of surrender.

If we ask "Who am I?" deeply and sincerely, the question eventually takes us to that place beyond all questions and answers. We approach the void where thoughts lose their significance, where the presence resides.

PART THREE
DARKNESS REVEALS THE LIGHT

*What we dislike most
can help us awaken.*

Chapter Ten
EMBRACING OUR FLAWS

Why is it that whenever I try hardest to be spiritual, I get bogged down in the worst aspects of my personality?

At the point in my life when I was most earnest about meditating, most determined to be loving and unattached, I saw my worst flaws magnified. First I noticed how angry I was. Then I saw how attached I was to material things. Later I became judgmental about how unspiritual I was. I wanted to be calm and detached, but I was anything but detached. Another driver would cut in front of me on the San Francisco–Oakland Bay Bridge and I'd honk my horn three or four times just to show my anger.

All my weaknesses surfaced at once—all my ugliest, most embarrassing traits. I was irritated by the most unlikely situations. As I rolled my cart down the aisle in Safeway, I felt annoyed at everyone—red-coated checkers at their cash registers, silver-haired women in pink polyester pantsuits, even toddlers gawking at boxes of Cheerios. I had no idea why I was so full of hostility.

Paradoxically, I found that the best way to deal with these flaws is to not do: to accept, to surrender.

It was a difficult time. My consumerism got out of control. Whereas before I'd only been mildly interested in cars, now I couldn't walk past a magazine rack without picking up a copy of *Road and Track* and thumbing through it for a glance at the new cars. At the very time I believed I was on a spiritual quest,

I found myself poring over an article titled "The Five Best Club Coupes You Can Own for Under $35,000"! I'd buy Sunday's *New York Times* just to look at ads for the latest computer monitors.

I longed to be spiritual, to feel Eternity's presence. But I was more full of desires and selfishness than ever.

When we see our flaws up close like this, we think we're not all right. So we do everything we can to change. We judge ourselves. We try hard, thinking that if we're diligent enough, we'll change. Paradoxically, I found that the best way to deal with these flaws is to *not* do: to accept, to surrender.

We start by experiencing the futility of trying to change. What is it like to surrender the need to control, to *not* try to figure everything out? How does it feel to admit that by ourselves we can't do anything—that we really can't change? What does it feel like to accept the hopeless feeling? Only when we've felt the hopelessness deeply are we ready for the next step: to accept our weakness, whatever it is. We welcome our fear, our anger, our need to run things.

At first it isn't easy to experience the hopelessness of trying to change. If for years we've been obsessed with improving ourselves, it's especially difficult to accept our flaws.

One evening several years ago, my wife and I were talking in the living room after dinner. At some point I began to advise her how she should expand her real estate business. I was sure my ideas were relevant. "You might want to consider calling those people from southern California," I said. My voice sounded reasonable and polite. But I was hiding my desire to control what she did. I assumed I knew what was best for her. Kat sensed the manipulation beneath the words. She scowled and said, "I don't want to hear what you think I should do." We argued. Our voices became louder and our conversation grew heated.

I had wanted to control things before, but I'd never *consciously* experienced that need. Now, I decided to embrace the controlling role that lay beneath my sensible facade.

I left the room and found a quiet place where I could be alone. Then I admitted to myself, "Yes, I

want to be in control. Hello, need-to-control." At
that moment I experienced the feeling of needing to
control things in my body. The muscles in my stomach felt tight. My jaw was rigid. "Yes," I blustered,
"I'm the boss around here. I feel the tyrant inside me,
the one who wants to be in charge." What a relief to
intentionally experience my need to dominate! In the
past I'd ignored it. Now I embraced that arrogant
part of my personality, the dictator role I'd never
admitted to before. In a few minutes my controlling
energy subsided. I grew calm and became aware of a
peaceful presence. There was no need to do anything
but let that presence work its will on me.

When I returned to Kat, we both realized that
the earlier upset was gone. She smiled as I reached
out and touched her shoulder. Having surrendered
my tyrant's posture, I sensed Eternity at hand. And
I saw that she did too. Though it's hard to put into
words, a special stillness arrived on the scene, a stillness that confirmed the presence was with us.

This incident and others like it have taught me
that if I consciously act out the controlling (or angry
or victim or fearful or shy) roles that I used to deny,

I let go of another small portion of the ego. I act them out alone—aware of the present, so I'm not lost in the roles.

———⋙•⋘———

She smiled as I reached out and touched her shoulder. Having surrendered my tyrant's posture, I sensed Eternity at hand. And I saw that she did too.

———⋙•⋘———

If, for example, I'm depressed because I feel distant from Eternity, I don't have to pretend everything is fine. I can experience the emptiness: "I feel miserable. How depressed can I let myself feel?" When I let the feeling unfold in this way, it usually turns out to be just another mood that comes and goes.

Shankara, the renowned Vedanta philosopher, once wrote that what is real is what lasts. From that perspective, our flaws have no enduring reality and are—like everything else in life—illusory.

꽃

THE WISDOM OF CONTRADISTINCTION

Once, when I asked a wise friend how I could get rid of my anger, I half expected him to reply, "Meditate on the Infinite and in time you'll become detached."

But instead he said, "You don't get rid of your anger. You welcome it!" He then explained an idea called *contradistinction:*

"You look at your anger, and you see the good in it," he said.

At first I didn't understand. "What do you mean, see good in anger?" I asked. "What's good about anger?"

"You look at the anger and greet it," he replied. Then illustrating, he said, "Hello anger, thank you for showing me what love is.

"What you're doing," he explained, "is seeing anger for its real role—showing you its opposite quality. You can't see a polar bear in a snowstorm, can you? White objects on a white background are invisible. The different hues help you distinguish things. Darkness makes the light clear. To see something, we need its opposite quality to make it distinct. It's the same with pain, sadness, grief, unhappiness, sickness—or anger. The negatives delineate their opposites."

———❖———

We would never recognize compassion, beauty, and calm if we weren't exposed to cruelty, ugliness, and storms. The tyrant helps us appreciate the saint.

———❖———

Contradistinction suggests that when we see a quality in ourselves we dislike, we thank it rather than judging, detesting, or trying to change it: "Hello fear, thank you for showing me what courage is." By acknowledging the negative's true role—to show us the good—we remove some of its power.

This means that we can use our least desirable qualities to learn about their opposites. When we feel sad, for example, we can use the sadness to understand joy. The same is true for hatred, which teaches us about love. We would never recognize compassion, beauty, and calm if we weren't exposed to cruelty, ugliness, and storms. The tyrant helps us appreciate the saint.

If we can experience our pain and upsets and welcome instead of avoid them, we can stop condemning ourselves. Rather than judging our flaws, we understand that they're transitory. In this way, our weaknesses act as guides to help us get out from under their grasp. But first we must be conscious.

As we begin to embrace what we used to view as our faults, we learn to love whatever comes our way. That's when we find Eternity's presence everywhere.

❧

Chapter Eleven
POWERFUL FEELINGS

For centuries, the great sages have urged detachment. They've warned of the pitfalls of getting lost in fear and rage, of getting ensnared by sensuality and greed. They've advised staying clear of worldly entanglements. "It is only when you stand back, remain detached in the midst of the passionate turmoil," says the contemporary Indian teacher Sri Aurobindo, "that you are able to see the process with a knowing eye."

The spiritual teachers caution us not to let our emotions run wild. Yet few say in detail what we can do with the feelings that sometimes control us. Some advise meditating and practicing yoga.

Others recommend contemplation, chanting, fasting, or prayer.

But no matter what we do, in the real world troublesome feelings, like mosquitoes that pester us on a muggy night, persist. The question remains: What do we do with the feelings that disturb the calm of our spiritual practice? If we're furious when someone slams into our car in a parking lot, does that mean we're somehow unspiritual? Or if we're terrified that one day the person we love most will abandon us, does our lack of detachment mean we're spiritually undeveloped?

I remember bickering with Kat one foggy summer evening in our San Francisco apartment. We fought for more than an hour, each of us convinced we were right:

"It's *your* fault. *You're* the one who started being distant!"

"But *you* make things much worse when you get so mad!"

I felt angry, frustrated we were still quarreling. We'd been in this situation before. For the first time I doubted we'd ever outgrow our fights. To make things worse, though I'd been meditating for years, I knew I was far from being the gentle person I wanted to be. At that moment, I felt terribly unspiritual.

I stormed down to the basement, into the big rectangular room where we stored old clothes and suitcases. I sat down. Something prompted me to ask, "What if, instead of expressing my anger to Kat the way I usually do, I explore the essence of the anger? What if I experience the anger physically— in my body—instead of trying to prove her wrong with logic?"

I imagined the fury within me: "Where, *exactly*, is it? Where?" I could feel it. It was there as tightness in my lower jaw, shoulders, and clenched hands. Then I exaggerated the tightness. "How intensely can I experience it?" I wondered. I kept this up for a minute or so, continuing to focus on my angry energy.

Suddenly I understood something that would transform my old ideas about how I could change. There was nothing I could do about the anger. There was nothing I could do about the senseless arguments or how hopeless they made me feel. Kat and I had already tried everything to stop arguing. We'd read the best-selling psychology books that described how to fight fair. We'd visited a couples therapist who taught us how to take responsibility by making I-statements. Things got better for a while. Then, sooner or later, we'd argue again, full of our passions of the moment, entwined in the tentacles of our combative egos.

Then, magically, a shift occurred. In an instant I realized that even if everything was hopeless, that was all right. If we were destined to argue forever, that, too, was all right. Hopelessness was fine!

I knew there was nothing we could do—nothing that would really change things. Right then I felt hopeless. Life felt hopeless. Everything felt hopeless.

Then, magically, a shift occurred. In an instant I realized that even if everything was hopeless, that was all right. If we were destined to argue forever, that, too, was all right. Hopelessness was fine! No longer did I need to control things. "Even if I'm in a relationship that right now feels impossible, that's okay," I thought. "I don't have to do anything about it. I accept things as they are."

Letting myself feel and accept that hopelessness was new for me. Right then I knew everything was proceeding perfectly. I'd given up on *doing* anything. At last I grasped the meaning of those words I'd heard so often but hadn't understood: "*Thy* will be done." Things weren't up to me. At that moment the gentle presence enveloped me. My need to shout, to confront, to prove Kat wrong was gone. In its place was love.

Yet this wasn't the love Kat and I felt for each other. Not romantic love. Nor was it sexual or platonic love. This was divine love, love that accepted me, despite my rancor, despite my contentious stance. This love allowed me to let go of my temper and welcome the presence. This was a love that existed beyond the realm of two human beings with their battling, self-righteous personalities.

Yes, my anger had left me! The feeling, which only seconds before had seemed so real, was gone. "Can it be that easy to get rid of anger?" I asked myself. I half-heartedly tried to evoke the original emotion: "No, it's all *your* fault," I imagined myself confronting Kat. "The problem is *you're* so dependent. *You're* the one who started it!" But my words sounded empty. The rage had vanished. Despite my effort to rekindle the feelings, I felt detached.

What happened was that for the first time I'd given up on arguing, given up on trying to be right. I'd even given up on trying to make sense out of things. Most important, I let myself physically experience the anger. As I did, its intensity faded. This act of letting go meant that my personality was no longer in charge. For the moment, I had surrendered the ego. And once surrendered, Eternity made its presence known.

Then I went upstairs and told Kat that I loved her.

Soon after that incident, I began to understand something else. The rancorous battles, the fiery disagreements, the conflicts that rage in the world—all come with the territory of being human. They're natural! They're supposed to be there! The ugliness of the upsets is there not to torment us, but to teach us about hopelessness: how to experience it, surrender into it, and then look beyond— to reality.

———————

This act of letting go meant that my personality was no longer in charge. For the moment, I had surrendered the ego. And once surrendered, Eternity made its presence known.

———————

I began to see the futility of scurrying about, constantly trying to manipulate what's wrong in life. This doesn't mean I sit back passive. I still do what

I can to try to change the things that look like they need changing. The part of me that's John Bailey living here in Minnesota hears from Amnesty International that a peasant from a Guatemalan village was abducted, then tortured by plainclothes police. That John Bailey still needs to fire off a letter to the Guatemalan president and police chief demanding they release their innocent prisoner. But I no longer pretend that John Bailey is "doing good." All those thoughts about me contributing to the world only end up expanding my ego. All the efforts, all the trying, though they may succeed in the short run, don't accomplish *lasting* change.

What a relief to realize that ultimately life is out of my hands—in the hands instead of the one who is the real source of hope. I finally understood that hopelessness *is* the fact of life; that real hope comes only from surrendering to that which lies beyond worldly appearances.

EXPERIENCING OUR EMOTIONS

Most of us grow up squelching our feelings. If it's drummed into us that only sissies cry, eventually we no longer cry. Or if we're hit whenever we're angry, eventually we may no longer consciously feel anger. Through these and other experiences of denying our feelings, it's not surprising that over time we lose touch with our emotions. With attentiveness and work, however, we can reclaim them.

The idea that it's good to experience our emotions isn't new, of course. For years psychotherapists have said that it's healthy to be in touch with our feelings. Progress in therapy is often measured by whether we can appropriately express anger, sadness, fear, and love.

But spiritually, there's a drawback to this emphasis on feelings. When I was in therapy, I constantly looked at how I felt. After years of negating my feelings, getting in touch with them made me feel affirmed and alive. That was beneficial. But it also meant that as much as ever things still revolved around me.

⇒◦⇐

In transcending feelings, the feelings themselves are only important as a first step in getting beyond them.

⇒◦⇐

In transcending feelings, the feelings themselves are only important as a first step in getting beyond them. The more we're limited to the "What am I feeling?" perspective, the more we believe that we—rather than the Infinite—matter. This is fine in psychotherapy when we need self-esteem. But the same approach that in therapy helps us combat neurosis, spiritually keeps us locked into an egotistical "I count" perspective.

If our aim is to grow spiritually by becoming more aware of the Infinite, we can take a step beyond being in touch with our feelings. We can surrender the feelings in the presence of the Eternal. We can transcend them. We do this by locating the source of the specific feeling and experiencing it. Then—and this is important—we allow that feeling to simply be there before the Divine.

FEELINGS AS TEACHERS

Years ago, when I read spiritual books that urged, "Be in the world but not of it," my feelings seemed much too intense. Yearning for serenity, I was anything but serene. Though I meditated every day, I didn't feel detached. I felt disturbed when I read about terrorist bombings. I felt sad when I'd see the stories on television about babies born addicted to cocaine.

Some of my feelings seemed hypocritical. "How," I asked myself, "can I think of myself as spiritual, yet so resent our sixty-five-year-old neighbor?" Doris left her television blaring *Gomer Pyle* reruns when she fell asleep drunk after midnight, while I lay awake fuming in the apartment next door. In those days I'd never considered using my angry feelings to remember Eternity's presence. Instead of being lost in my anger, I could have, as the next chapter shows, taken a minute or two to consciously feel it. By feeling it *consciously*, I mean feeling it intentionally, going right to its physical source. But back then I took my anger for granted. Convinced I was always right, I had no interest in examining my hostility. I didn't realize then how much it could teach me.

When I finally understood that I could transcend even my most intense feelings, my outlook on spiritual life shifted. No longer did I have to try to be calm. No longer did I have to dampen my intensity with constant meditation. Rather than making serenity the goal, I could let life's turmoil—in the form of powerful feelings—teach me. For years I'd viewed my intensity as a spiritual barrier. Now I see the opposite is true. If I experience my feelings with an awareness that the Infinite is at hand, they lead me to a place beyond feelings.

Feelings show us the ego in full bloom. They point directly to the desires and obsessions of an overblown ego. Experiencing our feelings and then letting them go allows us to bypass the logic of the intellect, the analysis of psychotherapy. When we surrender our feelings before Eternity, what's left is a gentleness that cradles us with love. When we consciously experience and surrender our feelings, they become reminders of God. Like the glint on a mine shaft wall that hints of inner treasures, feelings ultimately point us in the direction of the egoless diamond.

Chapter Twelve
TRANSCENDING FEELINGS

At first glance, the process of transcending feelings resembles what happens in psychotherapy. It differs, however, in three ways:

First, in transcending feelings, the emphasis is internal rather than external. Our aim is to experience the feelings within rather than to express them to someone. In her book *The Unmanifest Self,* Ligia Dantes lucidly sums up this approach with this question: "Have you ever challenged yourself to experience your emotions *totally* without any movement other than that of the inner emotional energy itself?"

Second, we turn our attention away from the feelings and place it instead on our awareness of the Eternal. We don't deny our feelings. We simply do what we did when we experienced glimpses: We shift our attention from the momentary feelings to a sense of being conscious of a witness being there with us.

Third, in going beyond feelings there's no need to analyze. Rather than figuring out why we feel what we do, we experience the feelings in the present—and transcend them.

You may find this idea of transcending feelings difficult at first. It's not always easy. To help me come into the presence, I devised the following exercise, influenced in part by the work of Fritz Kunkel, a leading proponent of depth psychology, and Eugene Gendlin, who wrote the 1978 book *Focusing*.

I. NOTICE AND LOCATE THE FEELING

The next time you're upset, find a quiet place where you can be alone. Try to get away from anything that distracts you. Start by asking yourself, "What do I feel?" Don't fall into the trap of focusing on what you think. ("I don't understand why Nancy doesn't love me.") Locate instead the *physical*

sensation in your body that accompanies your feeling. Exactly where is the feeling? Is it in your neck
or perhaps your stomach? Find its precise location.
Is it on the right or left side? Do you sense it's near
the surface of your skin or an inch or so beneath it?
Asking yourself these questions helps make your
feelings more concrete.

If it puts you more in touch with your feelings,
describe aloud what's happening. Try saying something like, "I'm devastated that she never wants to
see me again," or whatever fits your situation. Then
instead of keeping your attention on the words, shift
your awareness again to the feeling located in your
body. Can you pinpoint it? If you're angry, pay special attention to your jaw, your clenched hands, or
neck muscles. Or if you're afraid, your fear might lie
in a knot in your lower stomach.

Take a few minutes to notice the characteristics of
the feeling. Is it tingling or gnawing? Does your stomach feel like a taut rubber band? The more concretely
you experience the feeling, the better. Above all, don't
label it "wrong" or "inappropriate." Simply experience
it deeply without adding judgments.

Do you see the difference between *feeling* a knot of anger in your stomach and *thinking*, "He's a jerk"? Thinking about what we feel keeps us stuck in the neurotic thought, locked in judgments, trapped in a past and future that don't exist. Experiencing our feelings moves us through and beyond them.

II. INTENSIFY THE FEELING

Next, focus on the feeling. Experiment with exaggerating it. Give yourself permission to be outrageous if you wish!

At first this may be difficult. We often adopt quiet facades, hiding our feelings with reasonableness. But there's no need to play the appropriate grown-up now. If you feel self-righteous, play the indignant role to the hilt. Act logical to an extreme! Experience what it's like to judge rampantly, to offer pompous advice.

If you feel frightened, be afraid. Be that rejected one, the whiner, the one who whimpers and placates, who feels lost or deserted. If you feel selfish, be demanding. You don't need to be mature—no one will see you act like a seven-year-old brat! Forget about being spiritually evolved or whether you're in a state of higher consciousness. Be the essence of what it's like to be the worst brat imaginable! If this makes you self-conscious, remember that there's no one around to judge you. Only non-judgmental consciousness hears your intensity.

Fritz Kunkel describes an exercise of intensifying feelings before God in this way: "You hate your brother: imagine his presence, before God tell him how you feel, kick him, scratch him. You are ten years old now—get up from your chair, don't pretend to be a wise old Buddha, pace the floor, yell, scream, punch the furniture, express yourself. Rant and rage until you are exhausted, or until you laugh at yourself."

III. BECOME THE FEELING

By intensifying the feeling, you've made it more real. Now you're ready to become the feeling. *Be* the feeling rather than trying to do anything. If it's anger you're experiencing, instead of expressing anger *to* someone, become the quality of anger.

Imagine your body is the feeling. Rather than thinking, "I'm angry," be anger itself. Be the tightness of the anger rather than thinking an angry thought. If you're afraid, be the queasy knot in your stomach. Focus all of your attention there. For the time being, ignore everything else around you. Forget about the rug, floor, walls, and any background traffic noise. Don't listen to what your mind says. Be the feeling. Experience it fully!

IV. LOOKING BEYOND

Now comes the critical step—the one that takes you beyond your emotion to an awareness of the Infinite: transcending the feeling. Let yourself be aware that *something else is present*. Think of this something else as witnessing everything without judgment. This step requires becoming quiet and still, so you can notice any shift in perspective. It may help to imagine a witness who watches with you. What you call the watcher—God, Eternity, nature, or nothing at all—doesn't matter. What's important is that you know you aren't alone. You realize something divine is with you.

"In the presence of God, things change completely," writes Kunkel in describing this awareness. "Suddenly there's a sense of comfort and calm amid feelings that shortly before seemed so turbulent."

V. SURRENDER—THE PERSPECTIVE OF SOMETHING BEYOND

Now it's time to let go of the feeling. There's nothing you need to do or figure out. There's no need to worry. You're touching the hem of eternal essence by being willing to surrender. You don't have to *do* anything right. The universe doesn't fault you for being angry or fearful or dependent or self-righteous. You don't have to bow your head or say words written by saints or theologians. You don't have to imitate someone else's ritual. By being yourself before the one who already knows you better than you know yourself, you're in a state of openness, willing to allow whatever happens to happen.

———◆◇◆———

By being yourself before the one who already knows you better than you know yourself, you're in a state of openness, willing to allow whatever happens to happen.

———◆◇◆———

Within you is an awareness of something beyond. It has always been within you. Look to it as the presence that heals. Though you can't prove it scientifically, you *know* beyond any doubt that the Divine Watcher, God—whatever you want to call it—exists, even amid overwhelming feelings, even amid pain.

Chapter Thirteen
PAIN BRINGS US LIGHT

Two hundred years ago, French theologian Francois Fenelon put his finger on the nature of suffering. "We suffer," he wrote, "yet do not allow the mission of suffering to be accomplished in us." By this he didn't mean we should enjoy misery or that it's good to be in pain. What Fenelon meant was that *as long as we suffer anyway,* why not learn the lessons pain brings?

If, as the Buddha said, suffering is inherent in life, why go through the inevitable anguish—the cancers and heart attacks, the surgeries and hospital stays, the abuse, rejections and desertions, wars, and funerals, all to culminate in the certainty of watching our bodies wither and decay—without learning the lessons?

Most of us hate to feel grief, anguish, and despair. Nevertheless, something mysterious—even wondrous—happens if we *consciously* feel our pain. When we realize pain comes to us to be experienced rather than cast aside, then pain becomes our guide. No longer the villain, it shows us how to increasingly live in the presence.

Notice how Zen author Charlotte Joko Beck captures this idea of pain as a teacher in this passage from *Everyday Zen:* "My very difficulties in this very moment *are* the perfection," she writes. "We don't have to get rid of them, but we must see their nature. It's hard to get that we don't have to get rid of the calamity. The calamity is fine. We don't have to like it, but it's fine."

We usually respond to emotional pain by numbing ourselves to it. We'll do anything to avoid it. We all do this, believing we're not supposed to suffer. So we shunt the pain aside, pursuing endless ways to escape it. We swallow Prozac; sip beer, vodka, and chardonnay. We chain-smoke cigarettes or snort cocaine. We make pilgrimages to Disneyland and to Reno; go to parties, conventions, and cooking classes. We watch horror and adventure videos and keep track of trivia—runs batted in, yards rushed per game, or what Spock said to Kirk in the twelfth episode of *Star Trek*. We lose ourselves in science fiction and soap operas, in the images of Jungian archetypes. Or we follow the plot twists of *Masterpiece Theatre*, the nuances of a crisply phrased Haydn string quartet. We delve into past lives, prosperity, and channeled wisdom. Yet despite all our efforts to prevent pain, the suffering still lurks.

Some of us lessen the anguish by dwelling on the agony of others, poring over tabloids full of murder and mayhem. Or we're comforted by watching floods and airline disasters unfold on the evening news: "Did you hear about the 280 people who died on the jumbo jet that crashed out in Iowa? Terrible! And I thought *I* had it rough." If the pain of others is excruciating enough, it makes our own seem less severe. But although our pain is repressed, it's still there, pushed down so that we don't have to look at it. If we fail to avoid the pain, then we minimize it:

- "Think positive."
- "It's all for the best."
- "Don't worry, it'll turn out okay."
- "Put on a happy face."
- "There are others so much worse off."
- "I like to say the glass is half full—not half empty."

The positive-thinking approach—like the New Age affirmation that claims, "I'm already perfect just as I am"—may succeed in the short run. But at what cost? In the process of temporarily dampening our suffering, we cheat ourselves of the lessons pain brings. We never have a chance to discover pain's real purpose: to remind us of Eternity.

Often I forget about seeing pain as a teacher. Sometimes when I'm lonely, instead of sitting quietly and acknowledging my loneliness, I'll look for something to eat, a magazine to read, a news story to watch on television. When I'm unconscious, I'll do anything to avoid experiencing emptiness.

That's what most of us do with pain. We cast it aside. Instead of stopping long enough to experience our feelings, we worry and fantasize. We neurotically obsess about next month's audit or why our youngest daughter no longer calls. We think it's devastating that we lost our job. But we don't actually *feel* the feeling that plagues us. We *believe* we suffer. But we only fill our minds with thoughts that torment us!

———

*Only when we recognize its true role
as a teacher can pain show us how
to begin to awaken from the ego's grip.*

———

There is, however, a way to deal with pain so that rather than deadening us, it transforms us. But first we must realize that pain comes to us to be experienced. This understanding itself changes how we view pain. No longer the adversary we detest, it becomes our teacher. Only when we recognize its

true role as a teacher can pain show us how to begin
to awaken from the ego's grip.

EXPLORING PAIN'S ESSENCE

The last thing most of us want to do with our emotional pain is experience it. How rarely we say to ourselves when miserable, "I think I'll go into the core
of my pain. I'll go to the exact place where it hurts
most. Instead of thinking *about* the pain, I'll experience its full intensity." To many, such an approach
seems bizarre. Yet if we're open to its lessons, suffering shows us how to come into the presence.

Letting ourselves feel our suffering doesn't
mean we enjoy it. I still hate pain as much as anyone. My first attempts to let myself experience it
weren't easy.

In the days when the AIDS virus had just begun
to spread, the woman I was seeing at the time told
me that she'd gone out with a bisexual man a year
before. One February morning a few weeks after she
told me this, I woke up with swollen glands, feeling

exhausted. The left side of my face had broken out in a rash. "My God," I thought. "I could have AIDS." Frightful images filled my mind as I fantasized that my lungs would collapse, that my face would break out in lesions. I imagined that my body would deteriorate and that I'd soon die. These morbid thoughts disturbed me for days.

Then one evening, I made a discovery. Something prompted me to ask myself, "What's going on? Why don't you stop the paranoia and go into the pain instead? Explore what it's about. Feeling it couldn't be any worse than the thoughts you've had about it." It was true. Though I'd been in pain, the pain had been indirect. I hadn't *felt* it.

I decided to experience the pain, no matter what. I sat in a comfortable chair and let myself think of the images that obsessed me. But instead of staying with the thoughts, I put my attention on the constricted feeling *in my body*. "Just where is the pain?" I wondered. My upper body was tight and responded by constricting even further. I let the tightness intensify in my shoulders and chest. No longer was I immersed in thoughts about my suffering—I *felt* it. Next I opened myself to being the pain. I surrendered into it. It was as if something inside me said, "I give up. There's nothing I can *do* about it except experience it. It's in your hands now."

Up to this moment, the preoccupation with my pain wouldn't allow me to stop long enough to look beyond. Yet within a minute or two of surrendering, the frantic thoughts vanished. Everything seemed still. My focus shifted from my suffering to the Eternal. I sensed that a divine presence was with me, a presence that endured beyond my thoughts.

Once I finally surrendered into the pain, my neurotic fear of having AIDS left me. In its place was a calm inner knowing of that infinite reality that permeates everything. But before I could be aware of it, I had to be willing to feel the pain.

As a result of this and other distressing experiences, I've learned there's not much I can do about suffering—except feel it and surrender into it. Everything else—hating and minimizing it, ignoring and blaming others for it—is part of the strategy for avoiding it. At times, of course, we all naturally resist pain. But resistance only keeps us tight and constricted, shutting out another opportunity to remember Eternity.

Ultimately, this chance to remember Eternity is pain's real gift. Nevertheless, just because pain helps us experience God doesn't mean that we seek pain out or that we stay in an abusive relationship. We do what we need to do to get out of situations that harm us.

USING PAIN AS A TEACHER

Of all the things we can do on our spiritual journeys, viewing pain as a teacher is one of the most powerful. It's also one of the hardest. The following short exercise illustrates one way to consciously experience our pain:

Find a place where you can sit comfortably. Begin by thinking about something that makes you unhappy. Notice your painful thoughts. But instead of staying with the thoughts, watch how the pain expresses itself in your body.

Ask yourself, "At this moment, exactly where is this pain I've been avoiding? How deeply can I feel it *in my body?*" For now, forget about why the pain is there or what it means. Try to breathe easily. Go right into the essence of the pain. Experiment, if you wish, with allowing it to intensify. In most instances, the pain won't last more than a minute or two. Then allow yourself to let it go. What you're doing is surrendering. In essence you're saying, "Thy will be done. It's in your hands now."

⇒◦⇐

Of all the things we can do on our spiritual journeys, viewing pain as a teacher is one of the most powerful. It's also one of the hardest.

⇒◦⇐

You've just experienced the pain that you've tried to avoid. You've endured the worst of it—and you're all right! You're no longer shutting pain out, tightening your body, making your mind anxious. Exploring this painful feeling tangibly allows you to let go of the nagging thoughts so you can simply be.

Next, bring your awareness to a sense that a divine presence is there with you. For me, the Divine is gentle and subtle rather than vivid; it comes as a soft whisper rather than a blaring white light. But for each of us it's unique. Words cannot adequately describe this awareness. The only way to know it is to experience it. And you can!

Whenever we consciously feel our pain while remembering Eternity, awareness of the presence grows in us. And what was once pain, the unwelcome foe, increasingly becomes pain, reminder of the Infinite.

PAIN'S REAL ROLE

For years philosophers have known there is virtue in suffering. "The beliefs in duality, the misery, and brief pleasures had a purpose," writes David Manners in *Awakening from the Dream of Me*. "The anguish, the joy, the good, and the bad all brought me to where I am today. I give thanks for every depressing day of it!"

<hr>

But no matter how much we'd like
to live in a state of constant joy,
we all suffer. None of us is exempt.

<hr>

Nevertheless, most of us loathe pain. We instinctively do what we can to avoid it. Few among us set out jauntily for an appointment with the dentist for root canal surgery. We would all rather live a life free of burglaries and car wrecks, free of divorce, cancer, and death. But no matter how much we'd like to live in a state of constant joy, we all suffer. None of us is exempt. The one we love most dies or abandons us. The surgeon tells us a suspicious lump is malignant. We lose the job that sustains us. Or we become addicted to sex, drugs, or alcohol.

None of us seeks out pain. Yet pain comes our way. The pain is there in our feelings of anger, grief, rejection, or depression. It's there in knowing insecticides and other carcinogens poison our food supply. It's there in knowing we're in the midst of destroying our rain forests. It's there in knowing our bodies decay and succumb to disease. The pain is there in sensing the inevitability of our own deaths—and the deaths of everyone we love.

In the short run we have a choice. We can avoid pain or experience it. But in the end we need to experience life's suffering rather than escape it. If we merely repress it, pain returns, often in bigger doses. Ultimately, we learn pain's lessons. If we ignore them, they grow more dramatic. But over time we do learn.

Pain need not be catastrophic to teach us. Every upsetting situation can help us go beyond. Both the father who yells at us in an impotent rage and the supervisor who can only find fault give us a chance to go deeper. If we're awake to them, then even trivial incidents, such as dealing with a next-door neighbor whose dog howls at night, can remind us of the source.

———— ➤•◄ ————

When we allow ourselves to feel pain and then surrender into it, we stumble onto love. In this way, suffering shows us that the light we seek, rather than being external, is to be found within.

———— ➤•◄ ————

At first, suffering seems an unwanted intruder. But eventually pain prods us to grow beyond a viewpoint that cares only about what *I* want. If there were no pain, what incentive would we have to change? Without feelings of failure, sadness, humiliation, and abandonment, we'd remain stuck forever in our dramas, interested only in what makes us happy.

When we allow ourselves to feel pain and then surrender into it, we stumble onto love. In this way, suffering shows us that the light we seek, rather than being external, is to be found within. Pain's real intent all along has been to awaken us and point the way to oneness. In other words, even in difficult moments we can discover glimpses of the Divine. We can awaken to God by simply being ourselves.

Chapter Fourteen
ALREADY ON HOLY GROUND

Y ou don't have to be a monk, a metaphysician, or Mother Teresa to experience God's presence. Nor do you have to be somber, brilliant, or particularly pious. No credentials are required. Indeed, brain-power and religious titles only get in the way. Like a big bank account, they keep us believing in our own importance, bloating our egos while spiritually we remain numb.

We're aware of the presence not because we're perfect. There are no perfect human beings. Sooner or later we give up this idea that spiritual awakening belongs to a handful of kindly saints—we can be full of flaws and still experience it. For years we've been taught that we have to be disciplined or devout, but the need for religious accomplishment is a myth. Many who consider themselves religious have never known the presence. What matters is a growing awareness of the presence. That awareness is available to us all.

———⇒•⇐———

You don't have to be a monk,
a metaphysician, or Mother Teresa
to experience God's presence.
Nor do you have to be somber,
brilliant, or particularly pious.
No credentials are required.

———⇒•⇐———

For too long we've reserved the divine presence for a coterie of bishops and cardinals, *sadhus* and gurus, self-appointed preachers and brilliant philosopher-scholars—as if they were the guardians of *our* religious experience. Perhaps we believed we weren't smart, holy, or committed enough, or we presumed the core of spiritual life lay in some grand future awakening. But in waiting for the blinding light to find us, we ignored the tiny sparkle of a star in the night sky that could bring joy to the heart and help us remember the Divine.

In experiencing the presence, no event is too minute for our attention. We can be just as awake to that presence in the small appliance department at Kmart as in meditating in a perfect lotus. The potential for light is as present with mechanics amid the grease and grime of the neighborhood Amoco station as it is with Zen monks at a monastery in Kyoto. The possibility for awakening exists as much with the waitress who serves up a bacon cheeseburger at the Bun 'n Burger as it does with the Baptist minister who shouts, "Praise the Lord!" We can experience Eternity even if we've never heard of *karma* and *shakti,* even if we don't embrace angels, positive thinking, nondualism, channeled wisdom, or born-again experiences. We can experience it even if we're suspicious of religion—or of anyone who utters the word *God.*

While we can never prove the presence exists to others, we do know it when *we've* experienced it. And once experienced, there's no turning back. Once we recognize the presence is within and all around us, there's no reason to revere rituals and ceremonies, no need to bow down to human beings.

———⊰◦⊱———

Once we get away from our beliefs
of what is sacred and religious,
we finally grasp the meaning
of this wondrous journey:
to experience the presence and
awaken to our real identity.

———⊰◦⊱———

The great fifteenth-century Indian and Sufi poet Kabir made it clear that we're always in the presence in these vivid lines translated by Robert Bly:

Are you looking for me? I am in the next seat.
My shoulder is against yours.
You will not find me in stupas, not in Indian shrine
    rooms, nor in synagogues,
      nor in cathedrals:
not in masses, nor kirtans, not in legs winding
    around your own neck, nor in eating nothing but
    vegetables.
When you really look for me,
    you will see me instantly—
    you will find me in the tiniest house of time.
    Kabir says: Student, tell me, what is God?
    He is the breath inside the breath.

Once we get away from our beliefs of what is sacred and religious, we finally grasp the meaning of this wondrous journey: to experience the presence and awaken to our real identity. We experience this presence by surrendering, by relentless honesty, by *not* knowing.

When ordinary life becomes our guide, then every situation, every tiny thing that happens to us acts as our teacher. Even the most trivial interaction brims with potential for spiritual growth. Each moment gives us a chance to expand or to contract our awareness, to shower love on others or to turn inward. Every experience offers us a choice—we can remain egotistical or grow toward the Eternal. Everything helps us awaken. Everything confirms that we're already on holy ground.

Chapter Two
This Is It!

Page 27 *"It is a moment of relief..."*
William Samuel, "The Grandest Gift of All," in *Notes from Woodsong*, an unpublished newsletter (Birmingham, Ala., December 1988), 2.

Chapter Three
The Magic of Glimpses

Page 32 *"Moments like these..."*
Paul Brunton, *Inspiration and the Overself: The Notebooks of Paul Brunton*, vol. 14 (Burdett, N.Y.: Larson Publications, 1988), 117.

Page 43 *"My regiment was hit by..."*
William Samuel, *The Child Within Us Lives!* (Mountain Brook, Ala.: William Samuel Foundation, 1986), 17.

Chapter Four
RECOGNIZING GLIMPSES

Page 47 *"The dogwood tree was in full bloom . . ."*
> Amy Herrick, *At the Sign of the Naked Waiter* (New York: HarperCollins, 1992), 2.

Page 51 *"How do you know which foot . . ."*
> Walter Lanyon, *London Notes and Lectures* (London: Fowler and Co., n.d.), 72.

Page 51 *"The key is to be willing . . ."*
> Stephen Wolinsky, *The Tao of Chaos* (Bearsville, N.Y.: Bramble Books, 1994), 71.

Page 57 *"The only people who live comfortably . . ."*
> Charlotte Joko Beck, *Everyday Zen*, edited by Steve Smith (San Francisco: HarperCollins, 1989), 11.

Page 65 *"At the heart of every event . . ."*
> Karlfried Graf Dürckheim, *Dialogue on the Path of Initiation* (New York: Globe Press Books, 1991), 53.

Chapter Five
NOTICING THE SOUNDLESS SOUND

Page 68 *"Listen to the secret sound . . ."*
> Kabir, *The Kabir Book*, translated by Robert Bly (Boston: Beacon Press, 1977), 5.

Page 71 *"crystal-like vibration . . ."*
  Salim Michaël, *The Way of Inner Vigilance* (London:
  Signet Press, 1983; distributed by Element
  Books), 30.

Page 72 *"If we will but trust . . ."*
  Yogi Ramacharaka, *Advanced Course in Yogi Philosophy*
  (Chicago: Yogi Publication Society, 1931), 97.

Page 73 *"It is something to be experienced . . ."*
  Gyomay M. Kubose, *The Center Within* (Union City,
  Calif.: Heian International, 1986), 73.

Page 74 *"The sound of Being . . ."*
  Karlfried Graf Dürckheim, *Dialogue on the Path
  of Initiation* (New York: Globe Press Books,
  1991), 75.

Chapter Six
THE ME-SENSE

Page 78 *"How easy it is . . ."*
  David Manners, *Awakening from the Dream of Me*
  (Minneapolis: Non-Stop Books, 1987), 31.

Chapter Seven
LOOSENING THE EGO'S GRIP

Page 86 *"The ego is a strong and deadly serpent . . ."*
Shankara, *Shankara's Crest-Jewel of Discrimination,*
translated by Swami Prabhavananda and
Christopher Isherwood (Hollywood: Vedanta
Press, 1947), 82.

Chapter Eight
OVERCOMING JUDGMENTS

Page 99 *"Some people believe that if we let go . . ."*
Stephen Levine, *A Gradual Awakening* (New York:
Doubleday, 1989), 45.

Page 103 *"The best means of defusing the judging mind . . ."*
Levine, *A Gradual Awakening,* 46.

Chapter Nine
WHO AM I?

Page 111 *"When other thoughts arise . . ."*
Ramana Maharshi, *The Spiritual Teaching of Ramana
Maharshi* (Boston: Shambhala, 1983), 6.

Chapter Ten
Embracing Our Flaws

Page 125 *"You don't get rid of your anger ..."*
William Samuel, conversation with author, Birmingham, Ala., July 1987.

Chapter Eleven
Powerful Feelings

Page 129 *"It is only when you stand back ..."*
Sri Aurobindo, *Living Within: Selections from the Works of Sri Aurobindo and the Mother,* edited by A. S. Dalal (Ojai, Calif.: Institute of Integral Psychology, 1987), 26.

Chapter Twelve
Transcending Feelings

Page 143 *"Have you ever challenged yourself ..."*
Ligia Dantes, *The Unmanifest Self: Transcending the Limits of Ordinary Consciousness* (Boulder Creek, Calif.: Aslan Publishing, 1990), 81.

Page 147 *"You hate your brother ..."*
Fritz Kunkel, *Fritz Kunkel: Selected Writings,* edited, with an introduction and commentary by John A. Sanford (Mahwah, N.J.: Paulist Press, 1984), 287.

Page 149 *"In the presence of God, things change . . ."*
Kunkel, *Fritz Kunkel: Selected Writings*, 287

Chapter Thirteen
PAIN BRINGS US LIGHT

Page 151 *"We suffer, yet do not allow the mission . . ."*
Francois Fenelon, *The Choice is Always Ours: The Classical Anthology on the Spiritual Way*, edited by Dorothy Berkley Phillips (New York: HarperCollins, 1989), 188.

Page 152 *"My very difficulties in this very moment . . ."*
Charlotte Joko Beck, *Everyday Zen*, edited by Steve Smith (San Francisco: HarperCollins, 1989), 138.

Page 161 *"The beliefs in duality . . ."*
David Manners, *Awakening from the Dream of Me* (Minneapolis: Non-Stop Books, 1987), 56.

Chapter Fourteen
ALREADY ON HOLY GROUND

Page 171 *"Are you looking . . ."*
Kabir. *The Kabir Book*, translated by Robert Bly (Boston: Beacon Press, 1977), 33.

What gives a book the capacity to affect us, to reach us spiritually? For the most part, it has little to do with research or logic. The answer lies rather in whether it conveys an awareness of the presence.

If we approach spiritual books only with the intellect, we miss their import. We also miss the wonder of experiencing Eternity. Author David Manners puts it this way: "Words are not important," he writes. "It's what appears between them that sounds the bell and calls the unawakened to realization." In other words, an attitude of letting go is preferable to the diligence of a scholar.

Most of the books listed here (particularly in the "Eastern Philosophy" and "Christian Mysticism" sections), if approached gently and receptively, offer an understanding of Eternity that lies beyond the logic of the intellect.

Mentioned below are both Christian and Eastern works. Though to some their beliefs will seem contradictory, ultimately the differences are superficial, for the oneness they depict is identical.

❧

EASTERN PHILOSOPHY

Bankei. *The Unborn: The Life and Teachings of Zen Master Bankei.* Translated by Norman Waddell. Berkeley, Calif.: North Point Press, 1984.

> *Zen philosophy in its most readable form. Instead of stories and koans to confound the intellect, seventeenth-century Zen Master Bankei offers simple words directed to the heart. "You can grasp your Buddha-mind very easily, right where you sit, without that long, punishing practice," says Bankei (p. 80).*

Kabir. *The Kabir Book.* Translated by Robert Bly. Boston: Beacon Press, 1977.

> *Irreverent, passionate verse from the Hindu mystic poet who lived during the fifteenth century: "Are you are looking for me? I am in the next seat. . . . You will not find me . . . in synagogues, nor in cathedrals: not in masses . . . nor in eating nothing but vegetables" (p. 33).*

Maharaj, Nisargadatta. *Awaken to the Eternal.* Encinitas, Calif.: Inner Directions, 1995. Videocassette.

> *This recent video provides the only film footage available of contemporary sage Maharaj. It includes interviews with Jack Kornfield, Jean Dunn, Robert Powell, and Stephen Wolinsky.*

————. *I Am That: Talks with Sri Nisargadatta Maharaj.* Translated by Maurice Frydman. Edited by Sudhakar S. Dikshit. Durham, N.C.: The Acorn Press, 1986.

A simple tobacco merchant from Bombay who died in 1976, Nisargadatta Maharaj espouses the philosophy of nondualism. This sometimes difficult work from a great contemporary teacher offers absorbing insights for readers interested not just in logic, but in that which lies behind logic.

Maharshi, Ramana. *The Collected Works of Ramana Maharshi.* Edited by Arthur Osborne. York Beach, Maine: Samuel Weiser Inc., 1970.

A carefully edited collection of the sage's original works. This comprehensive survey of his non-dualistic philosophy (Advaita Vedanta) includes a thorough exposition of Maharshi's discipline of Self-inquiry.

————. *The Spiritual Teaching of Ramana Maharshi.* Boston: Shambhala Publications, 1988.

These dialogues in question-and-answer form offer an overview of his philosophy. Jung's introduction emphasizes how teachers like Ramana Maharshi have much to show the West about developing the inner life.

————. *Talks With Ramana Maharshi*. Available through Inner Directions, PO Box 231486, Encinitas, CA 92023 (800 545-9118).

> *This is the most comprehensive record we have of the transcribed words of the famous Hindu teacher. Dozens of ordinary people ask Maharshi a wide range of questions about their immediate concerns.*

Rumi, Jelaluddin. *Daylight*. Translated by Camille and Kabir Helminski. Putney, Vt.: Threshold Books, 1990.

> *Transcendent poems that speak directly to the heart from the legendary Sufi mystic. Practical wisdom and love of God permeate his words (p. 110):*
> > *Little by little God takes away human beauty:*
> > *little by little the sapling withers . . .*
> > *Seek the spirit;*
> > *don't set your heart on bones.*

Shankara. *Shankara's Crest-Jewel of Discrimination*. Translated by Swami Prabhavananda and Christopher Isherwood. Hollywood: Vedanta Press, 1978.

> *Written in the eighth century by the eminent Indian philosopher, Shankara, this is a succinct, highly read-able introduction to the Vedanta path to God through knowledge.*

❦

CHRISTIAN MYSTICISM

Chapman, John. *Spiritual Letters*. London: Sheed and Ward, 1935.

> *A pragmatic guide to spiritual life from one of England's most renowned religious scholars. Full of useful advice with frequent references to Jean Pierre de Caussade.*

de Caussade, Jean-Pierre. *Abandonment to Divine Providence*. Translated by John Beevers. New York: Doubleday, an Image Book, 1975.

> *An unpretentious, invaluable work that focuses on using the present moment and total surrender of the will as ways to approach God.*

Eckhart, Meister. *Meister Eckhart*. Translated by Raymond B. Blakney. New York: Harper and Row, 1941.

> *A compilation of the legendary fourteenth-century mystic-scholar's twenty-eight most well-known sermons.*

Fenelon, Francois. *Fenelon's Spiritual Letters*. Beaumont, Tex.: Seedsowers, 1982.

> *During the seventeenth century, Fenelon, archbishop of Cambrai, wrote these letters outlining the basic principles of spiritual life. Offers a remarkably clear explanation of the role of suffering in spiritual life.*

Johnston, William, ed. *The Cloud of Unknowing and The Book of Privy Counselling*. New York: Doubleday, an Image Book, 1973.

> *The first title is one of the most popular of early Christian mystical works. The second,* The Book of Privy Counseling, *is only forty pages long and relatively unknown. Its anonymous author spells out how loss of ego is the key to enlightenment.*

Lawrence, Brother. *The Practice of the Presence of God*. Translated by John J. Delaney. Foreword by Henri Nouwen. New York: Doubleday, an Image Book, 1977.

> *A spiritual classic that describes the discipline of humbly remembering God's presence in every activity throughout each day.*

Molinos, Michael. *The Spiritual Guide*. Auburn, Maine: Christian Books, 1982.

> *Molinos, the persecuted Spanish priest and mystic, was condemned as a heretic to a life sentence by the Inquisition. His writings look at the distinction between meditation and contemplation, between external activity and the inner way.*

Tauler, Johannes. *Johannes Tauler: Sermons*. Translated by Maria Shrady. Mahwah, N.J.: Paulist Press, 1985.

> *An influential German mystic, Tauler shows how in spiritual life experience takes precedence over book learning: "You must put aside all rational methods, for reason is now beneath you, and then you may become united with the One" (p. 105).*

CONTEMPORARY

Beck, Charlotte Joko. *Everyday Zen*. Edited by Steve Smith. New York: HarperCollins, 1989.

> *Beck takes the subtleties of Zen philosophy and puts them into practical, modern terms. A valuable, common-sense approach to spiritual awakening.*

Brunton, Paul. *Inspiration and the Overself: The Notebooks of Paul Brunton,* vol. 14. Burdett, N.Y.: Larson Publications, 1988.

> *This is only one of twenty-eight Brunton notebooks that delve into every aspect of spiritual life. Chapters 4 through 8 (pp. 109–252) include a comprehensive examination of glimpses and their significance.*

Goldsmith, Joel S. *A Parenthesis in Eternity.* New York: Harper and Row, 1963.

> *This lucid introduction to some of the deeper mysteries of metaphysics is written by one of the twentieth century's most widely read spiritual authors—Joel Goldsmith.*

———. *Practicing the Presence.* New York: Harper and Row, 1958.

> *The introduction and final chapter of* Practicing the Presence *offers a unique explanation of what it means to be in the presence.*

Klein, Jean. *The Ease of Being.* Durham, N.C.: The Acorn Press, 1984.

———. *Neither This Nor That I Am.* Somerset, England: Watkins Publishing, 1981.

————. *Who Am I? The Sacred Quest.* Edited by Emma Edwards. Dorset, England: Element Books Limited, 1988.

> *A European musicologist and doctor, Jean Klein's philosophy belongs to the tradition of Advaita Vedanta or the way of knowledge. His words point to the state of no-mind, to the Infinite: "There is no system, method or technique by which to approach reality. It reveals itself when all techniques and systems fail and the futility of volition is seen. Then the mind comes into a state of innocent surrender"* (The Ease of Being, *p. 27*).

Samuel, William. *The Child Within Us Lives!* Mountain Brook, Ala.: William Samuel Foundation, 1986.

> *A comprehensive work that integrates Western psychology and philosophy with Eastern metaphysics. Samuel shows how discovery of the Inner Self (he wrote about "the child within" long before it become a popular psychology cliché) leads to spiritual transformation. Includes chapters on glimpses, transcending dualism, and living subjectively in an objective world.*

————. *A Guide to Awareness and Tranquillity*. Mountain Brook, Ala.: William Samuel Foundation, 1967.

> *A good introduction to the core of Samuel's early teachings. He approaches philosophy from the subjectivist perspective: "The world is not as it appears to the busy, troubled mortal . . . perfection permeates everything."*

PSYCHOLOGY

Gendlin, Eugene T. *Focusing*. New York: Bantam Books, 1988.

> *This popular, innovative work ventures beyond the usual analysis of feelings found in psychology books. Illustrates by specific example how readers can concretely experience feelings directly within the body.*

Kunkel, Fritz. *Fritz Kunkel: Selected Writings*. Edited by John A. Sanford. Mahwah, N.J.: Paulist Press, 1984.

> *At a time when most psychoanalysts contended "the very idea of God was a childish illusion perpetuated by mankind for neurotic reasons," depth psychologist Kunkel openly wrote about God's presence. His contribution to the study of psychology is unique: he combines psychological techniques with a spiritual perspective in working with personal crisis. Kunkel stresses that the real healer is already within us.*

asana	A bodily posture, usually associated with *hatha yoga*
ashram	A place where spiritual seekers gather
chakra	Energy center in the human body
jnana-yoga	The path of knowledge or of the intellect, considered one of the most difficult Eastern paths
koan	Nonsense question posed by a Zen teacher to student in order to encourage an expanded awareness of reality
kundalini	Means "snake." Refers to the spiritual energy said to lie coiled at the base of the spine of every human being. Kundalini *yoga* aims at awakening this energy

om	Sacred sound of the universe
sadhu	Hindu holy man
shakti	A force or energy. Some spiritual groups believe this force is transmitted by their gurus
siddhi	Supernatural or spiritual powers
Vedanta	Hindu philosophy of non-dualism
vichara	The process of self-inquiry often associated with Ramana Maharshi
yantra	A geometrical diagram used as an icon in meditation

J. K. Bailey began his spiritual journey twenty years ago practicing transcendental meditation and studying the writings of Krishnamurti. Over time, the pilgrimages, meditative techniques, and philosophy that became part of his quest gave way to a simple awareness of being in the presence.

A former New Yorker and graduate of Trinity College in Connecticut, Bailey is a longtime writer. After working as a copywriter in Manhattan, he moved to California and wrote a guidebook to the Bay Area titled *The San Francisco Insider's Guide*. Recently, he edited and published *Awakening from the Dream of Me*, a book about spiritual awakening by David Manners. He's just completed a humorous book about food and is now working on a second book on spirituality.

Bailey lives near Minneapolis with the woman he's married to, Kat Bourque.